4

Harold Kaplan

Power and Order

*Henry Adams and the
Naturalist Tradition in
American Fiction*

The University of Chicago Press
Chicago and London

Harold Kaplan is professor of English and acting
chairman of the Department of English at Northwestern University. His previously published works
include *Democratic Humanism and American
Literature*.

The University of Chicago Press, Chicago 60637
The University of Chicago Press, Ltd., London

Printed in the United States of America
6 5 4 3 2 1   81 82 83 84 85

Library of Congress Cataloging in Publication Data

Kaplan, Harold, 1916-
   Power and order.

   Includes index.
   1.   American fiction—19th century—History and
criticism.   2.   Naturalism in literature.   I.   Title.
PS374.N29K36   813'.009'12   80-23414
ISBN 0-226-42424-3

For learning,
to my mother and to Raymond Sanford

Contents

Preface

To treat of the relation between literature and politics has its obvious dangers, apart from the risk of becoming easily drowned in controversy. Even the most sophisticated political theory works at odds with the literary imagination, for discursive politics has an irrepressible tendency to create abstractions, while any literature of merit moves almost always toward the rejection or revision of those general ideas that have entered the public domain as stereotypes.

This is a warning to be kept in mind by all students who engage in the project of seeing literature from the perspective of politics. It seems to me, however, that the reverse way of putting the issue helps toward the solution of the difficulties. To see politics from the perspective of literature is to find the ground where they actually coexist, that is, where they share a source in cultural myth. Modern theoretical politics in the West has been led by an ambition to achieve metaphysical status and philosophic universality. At least since the democratic revolutions of the eighteenth century, ideologies have taken on the character of secular religions, and the strongest political currents of this century and the last have surely confirmed and heightened that development. Marxism, for instance, as generally practiced and as it has influenced intellectual life, has made as wide a claim for relevant authority in all spheres of human existence as any universalist myth or dogma that we know, including that of the Virgin of Chartres, even as she was drawn in Henry Adams's imaginative portrait of her and her civilization. This is again to suggest that the politics that meets literature on the deepest level, beyond mere description or propaganda, is a metapolitics, one founded on premises that link nature and human history and approach teleological design.

I was drawn to the study of American naturalist fiction written at the turn of the century exactly because it offered an unusually instructive example of how such a system of thought, founded on neoscientific premises and offering neopolitical conclusions, could affect the literary imagination. The works of Dreiser, Crane, and Norris that I treat here were all published within a period of eight years, beginning in 1893, with Crane's *Maggie,* and ending with

Norris's *The Octopus* in 1901. *Mont-Saint-Michel and Chartres* and *The Education of Henry Adams* were privately printed by Adams in 1904 and 1906. The likelihood that Adams read none of the novels only supports the sense that the affinities between him and the novelists run deeper than topical interests and outweigh temperamental differences. Adams would surely not have appreciated Dreiser's writing as fiction, and Norris, though probably the closest to Adams in an ideological sense, was the furthest from him in style and character. As for Crane, one can imagine Adams recognizing another ironic spirit.

Decidedly, however, when we encounter the dry brilliance of Adams's constantly alert spectatorial intelligence and the stoicism superimposed on his deep sense of moral defeat, we think of him as closer to the modernist generation than to the early disciples of Zola and Spencer in this country. He was a man who placed himself at the fulcrum of change, facing large historic transitions. His moral roots were, as he said, in the eighteenth century; he was vividly responsive to the intellectual weather of the nineteenth; and he prophesied with great accuracy for the twentieth. He made himself the alienated heir of American history and the disillusioned conscience of democracy. Yet everyone knows that Adams's famous "failure" was his real success and that one of the ways in which he succeeded in failure was as a system-maker without a system, a man with a self-mocking but real ambition to translate science, history, modern politics, and economics into a unified view of the world. In effect, his compulsive interest in science, his fascination with the struggle of social "forces," his deep inherited respect for power in all its human and natural manifestations, gave his writing a unity like the unity he longed for and found missing in the actual civilization he knew. Adams expressed the naturalist imagination working at the margin of questioned values and struggling to create a mythology and ethos to guide human existence. For this reason his works provide a background of coherence that brings out the sharpest implications in the work of his contemporary generation of fiction writers.

There is a tendency among critics and students to think of literary naturalism as a closed chapter of modern literary history, except for some archaic survivals. That is wrong on two counts, one of them being the obvious point that much modernist writing, whether called "symbolist" or "expressionist," "subjective" or "surreal," found its creative energy by reacting against the stylistic and philosophic implications of naturalism. Yet, much deeper than the negative differences, there is a continuity in modern imaginative culture with the work of the naturalists. Our understanding of these literary traditions is greatly enriched when we find, as I propose, that the major literary contribution of naturalist thought is a myth of power and conflict charged with apocalyptic themes of order and chaos, creation and destruction, purgative crisis and redemptive violence.

Apart from literature—for in this case literature has followed titanic masters—the significance of that naturalist myth and ethos cannot fail to be recognized. Twentieth-century history has laid down a terrible record of the existence of a culture of power and struggle, a culture deeply fatalistic, relying on historic process, and disciplined to stoicism by its awareness of natural strength and the inevitability of suffering. The issue is normative, and, if the dominant thought of our era is naturalistic, as most would agree it is, then what we are dealing with, far beyond the realms of literature, is a normative naturalism affecting all our views of human character and values. If, at the level of primordial beginnings and apocalyptic endings, force seems to meet force in fateful process—if that is all there is for judgment—then the response to force defines value.

In the last analysis, even the rage for order, whether in art or in the art of politics, concedes a great point to nature's power and its threat of chaos. Without generalizing too much about either art or politics, one might suggest that students focus on how the imagination functions in crisis, surrounded by blank surfaces and impulses of energy in a world where, as Wallace Stevens once said, reality has become violent and the imagination is obliged to summon a form of violence in resistance.[1]

I wish here to express my debt to those people and agencies who have helped me in my work. Northwestern University has been generous with leave from teaching. The National Endowment for the Humanities supported this work with a grant for the summer of 1977. My colleagues in the English Department at Northwestern, Gerald Graff, Joseph Epstein, and Carl S. Smith, read and criticized important parts of the manuscript. Mary Penchoff and Marjorie Weiner helped efficiently with its preparation.

An earlier version of chapter three, "The Metapolitics of Henry Adams," appeared in *Social Research* 46 (Autumn 1979).

1 The Myth of Power

The assumption guiding my study and a large area of literary interpretation could be stated in some blunt words of Anthony Burgess's. "Literature," he said, "is recognizable through its capacity to evoke more than it says . . . [it] suggests a theology or metaphysic of which the story itself is a kind of allegory."[1] One thinks, yes, a serious literature does evoke large-scale meaning in this sense, and modern writing in particular has, since the turn of the century, seemed to act in unique concert in reaching toward allegory. The better term for so weighty a suggestiveness might be myth, but, in any case, if there are metaphysical allegories in modern literature of the kind implied by Burgess, we would not look for their source in theology. Henry Adams, an intellectual amateur in many fields but preeminently a man of letters, leads the way for my study in finding in science the modern inspiration for metaphysical language and story. The bridge to the humanities from science was direct in his case but was multiplied many times by intermediate passages through politics and social thought. In this he was most characteristic, long before Bertrand Russell made the theme his own at the outset of his book entitled *Power*, where he said,

> I shall be concerned to prove that the fundamental concept in social science is Power, in the same sense in which Energy is the fundamental concept in physics.[2]

So simple an observation seems obvious, yet its really awesome implications for practical behavior and imagined values in our culture have been relatively neglected, possibly because those who study culture are often the ones most dominated by Russell's premise. It is for the latter reason that I feel confident there are important discoveries to be made beyond the confines of this study. I search for the expressive qualities of a myth of power or what can be called a metapolitics of conflict and power. Our century's claim on metaphysical and moral inspiration has its root in the nineteenth, when scientific positivism first became the breeding ground for interpretive allegories in politics. The concept of power, as Russell suggests, had its source in physics but found its

1

chief resting place in the political and economic ideologies that dominate two centuries.

A sensitive judgment of this major transition in normative thought came from George Santayana, who, though he called himself a skeptic and a naturalist, spoke soberly of what he saw as the mistaken effort to encode values on the terms of natural existence.

> Religion may falsely represent the ideal as a reality, but we must remember that the ideal, if not so represented, would be despised by the majority of men, who cannot understand that the value of things is moral, and who therefore attribute to what is moral a natural existence, thinking thus to vindicate its importance and value. But value lies in meaning, not in substance; in the ideal which things approach, not in the energy which they embody.[3]

Much of the program of modern critical realism and naturalism in literature could be described as the systematic exposure of idealities that are false, demonstrably unrelated to "natural existence." But more deeply, and extending far beyond the conventional definition of literary naturalism, there is an ethos, perhaps the strongest semblance of one in modern writing, which must be understood as the effort to value things for the energy they embody.

Obviously this could not occur without a great shock to the traditional ethical wisdom. Julien Benda was a more committed moralist and man of faith than Santayana, and so he reflects the change more sharply and as a matter of controversy. In doing so he is also closer to the active spirit in modern literature:

> It is impossible to exaggerate the importance of a movement whereby those who for twenty centuries taught Man that the criterion of the morality of an act is its disinterestedness, that good is a decree of his reason insofar as it is universal, that his will is only moral if it seeks its law outside its objects, should begin to teach him that the moral act is the act whereby he secures his existence against an environment which disputes it, that his will is moral insofar as it is a will "to power," that the part of his soul which determines what is good is its "will to live" wherein it is most "hostile to all reason," that the morality of an act is measured by its adaptation to its end, and that the only morality is the morality of circumstances.[4]

Benda's statement can serve well as my introduction, because he was one of the first to realize that modern naturalism would breed moral systems, determining "what is good" according to the norms of power, circumstance, and the "will to live." As he said, this was a turning point "in the moral history of the human species," but his theme has not been sufficiently heard for the simple reason that most naturalist thought is regarded not as moralizing but as the stoic effort to teach harsh truths. However, in the literature influenced by naturalism the principles Benda describes are clearly visible as normative, myth-making standards.

One could emphasize the historic reversal by illustrations taken from the myth of the genesis of morals, which forms the substance of Aeschylus's Prometheus trilogy. In that work Aeschylus developed a legend of the progressive moral education of the gods, which brought their purposes into harmony with the interests of humanity. Zeus, at the beginning of the story, rules the universe with the aid of his daimons, Might and Violence. Prometheus, bound on his rock, has played the crucial role in defense of man, opposing force with intelligence, the arts of civilization, and the sense of justice. The one surviving play of the trilogy predicts a future accommodation between the sovereign power of Zeus and the values Prometheus defends, one that will usher in the essential story of civilization.

The modern myth of power reverses the narrative logic of Aeschylus's story and tells the determinative story of civilization in terms of conflict relationships and power realities. The world turns back to its primitive origins, and the only gods are Titans. The story of the pre-Olympians seems intended to shock the idealizing imagination of the Greeks with the most abrupt and savage contrasts. Cronus, for instance, was the Titan overthrown by Zeus, his son, as he himself had overthrown and then castrated his father, Uranus. He also met his sister in incest and climaxed his unrestrainedly primitive behavior by cannibalizing his own children.

Such a legend of genesis is a most impressive reading of the primordial human condition, and there will always be something ambiguous in its juxtaposition with civilized standards. However brave the defense of the latter, they take on exactly a defensive quality when the authority of science, whether in biological evolution, in anthropology, or psychology, is constantly evoked in comparisons of the primary and the secondary, the natural and the invented, the "raw and the cooked." My theme in this book begins at this point, where the effort is made to coopt the revelations of science, or naturalist truth, on behalf of overt or covert values. Cronus becomes a teacher more instructive than Prometheus, for the task is not directly that of achieving freedom and justice but a maneuver by which the monster god becomes tamed through the displacement, transference, or sublimation of the violent natural powers he represents.

In the effort to understand the necessary reductivism of a science-dominated culture, we must begin with its vocabulary, where, as Bertrand Russell suggests, the word of greatest importance is "power." Another is "order," which, in this context, most simply means control of power. Other words are "force," "energy," "conflict," "struggle," "unity," "chaos," "destruction," "violence," "birth," "growth," "decline," and "death." It would be a study of some worth to examine the frequency and the relationships of the words of that vocabulary in literary, scientific, and political writing as well as in popular journalism and entertainment. I limit myself here to a few texts from the literature of America in the early twentieth century, a crucial period in a most significant place; but it is in literature, even minor literature, that the unmeasured implications of a deep system of belief, a myth, become accessible.

The language of power, whether it forms a myth, a metaphysics, a political ideology, or a broad imaginative tradition, can best be located in the work of an early generation of philosophic naturalists and vitalists, among them Marx, Spencer, Nietzsche, Bergson, Zola, and Sorel, all of whom made partial contributions. Although they do not, of course, share a single system, they illustrate a general process of adapting human values to naturalist realities, a process that resulted in covert forms of a naturalist ethic. The passive tendency of a normative realism, I suggest, was to submit to whatever has unassailable existence and unmistakable force. The active alternative to this passivity was a cult of power in which the manifestations of energy and force became awesome signs, sources of true revelation. Conflict was the locus of the chief ritual or practical demonstration of power, and conflict therefore became subject to metaphysical and teleological interpretations, such as the Darwinian theme of natural selection or the Marxian theme of political evolution and redemption. Dramatic values were found in apocalyptic crises of ultimate violence or in the fateful cycle of decline and ascent. These ordeals of fate and violence provided the determinant revelations of historic success or failure, and in personal drama they provided revelations of personal worth. But personal values, at least for the first generation of naturalists, were hardly describable except in terms which reflect biological and political values. The overall literary effect was to subordinate the action of individuals to social process and the character of individuals to the identity of groups.

This, then, is the formula with which I begin. My method, however, is dialectical; it is the distinctions and oppositions among naturalist themes, not their uniformity, that has application to literary subjects. I have limited these subjects to Henry Adams and a number of American fiction writers of the first decades of the twentieth century in order to confine within reasonable limits an almost limitless theme and to provide the most meaningful context of rival traditions, humanist and idealist, in American writing. I start with an extended discussion of Henry Adams's two major works, conceiving him as a focus for the radical change of consciousness that naturalism effected in America and judging also that he may have the significance for future students that Emerson now has for us in representing his own and later generations of American writers. I go on with a study of the primary American naturalists in fiction, the contemporaries of Adams's old age: Dreiser, Crane, and Norris. I add Dos Passos to that discussion to indicate the bridge with the continuing naturalist orthodoxy without giving further historical review to writers like Farrell, Steinbeck, the early Norman Mailer, and James Jones and the now obscure and unread school of "proletarian" or Marxist novelists. My approach is topical and intensive, and so the themes of my study should suggest their relevance and value to the larger naturalist tradition. But they also provide, as I suggest throughout the text, an illuminating path of reference to the later modernists, Hemingway, Fitzgerald, and Faulkner, who deviate in sharp ways from literary naturalism but whose work cannot be deeply understood without reference to the philosophic context of naturalism and to what I have called the metaphysics of power.

Naturalism remains a useful term for describing a literary practice and a set of programmatic ideas reflecting the laws of thermodynamics, Darwinian theory, and the sociological thought derived from Adam Smith, Malthus, Marx, and Spencer. Nevertheless, any literary tradition that is serious will tend to reject intellectual conformity and be concerned primarily with the dramatic problems generated by the literary imagination. Much that is most significant in the original school of ideological naturalist writing survives in the later generation: the awesomeness of power and its revelations, themes of victimization and passivity, a special concern with the rituals of violence, and the brooding, oppressive sense of naturalist fatality. All this becomes stronger, more sharply accented, because the role of reactive consciousness and response is restored to classic standing. Orthodox or conventional naturalism tended to bury individual response in the stream of causality or to identify the force of human agents with the generalized force of history or nature. Whether realist or antirealist, and whatever the philosophic bias, the later fiction tends to focus on the grandly equivocal issue of conscious freedom, testing qualities of response to the hard neutrality of being and its force and questioning the moral authority of nature. It is possible to say that for the early naturalists nature's authority was absolute and that the work of Dreiser compares with Emerson's as the naturalist inversion of transcendental idealism. But to show a most important development, the work of Faulkner compares with Melville's in returning to the classic existential drama of the ethical will. The writing of Hemingway would add illustration of an intense pathos, relieved by the stoic half-victories of personal bearing, endurance, and awareness. What is fascinating, difficult, and "modernist" in the work of both Faulkner and Hemingway centers on the ordeal of the normative imagination, committed to naturalist revelations yet at odds with them, extracting the deepest lessons from nature yet refusing to remain its mere human function and expression.

The American Context

The authority of the eighteenth-century democratic revolutions, in America as well as France, was based on a most daring effort to link ethical and naturalistic truths. In natural-rights theory, democracy gains support from nature for the two basic ideals of equality and freedom. Equality cannot be demonstrated from the experience of social or acculturated man. Quite the opposite: intrinsic equality has to preexist known human societies, at least conceptually, and be the objective to be regained in revolutionary or reformist societies. In the same vein of Enlightenment thought, natural freedom is the accompaniment of natural reason; it is the medium in which reason can function, just as reason is required for the success of freedom. The human capacity for reason guarantees that free acts will harmonize with the rational structure of the universe. And it is reason, as Thomas Paine proclaimed, that is the chief resource against superstitious and traditional authority.

Transcendentalism and the American versions of romantic naturalism were even more absolute for freedom. Here freedom is the function of consciousness and inspiration. Human spirit responds to the spirit in nature, to assure an ultimate harmony between the profound motives of men and the design of things. The more free, the more connected with nature, Emerson would say. The more willing the mind is to entertain the "soul," or consciousness, the more closely it is linked with reality. And the more personal and individual the source of inspiration, the more authentic is its realistic authority.

This was an intellectual tour de force by which subjectivity and individualism not only were harmless but were welcomed for their ability to establish communication with actual nature or with the spirit in nature and the spirit in other people. That romantic faith was more extreme in America than elsewhere because a democratic culture already felt threatened by the increasingly strong determinism of science and the amoral realities of business and politics. The primacy of persons was being opposed by concepts of group power and social process, and the species language of Darwin and Marx was only a few years away from its triumph. The method of science, of categorical statistics and empirical history, was threatening to isolate all subjective experiences, particularly those of the imaginative conscience, and denigrate them as anthropocentric solipsism. But democracy was impelled by the primacy of the individual conscience and the privileges granted to it in the name of that primacy. This conscience guarded not only the franchise but free expression; and if the authority of conscience were threatened, who could imagine the consequences for a democratic culture?

For these reasons the study of modern naturalism assumes particular importance in the history of a democratic country and its literature. To understand the tensions within the tradition, we should examine the most extreme contrast possible, with Emerson at one end of the nineteenth century and Theodore Dreiser at the other. Emerson was quite consciously a man of the pulpit, with secularizing impulses; he was really as bold as Whitman in the latter's pronouncement, "The priest departs, the divine literatus comes." Indeed, the secret of the surviving vigor of Emerson's work lies in the unrestrained zest of his anthropomorphic spirit. The God he reverenced was incarnate in his own skin; he could assume that the same God listened in others as he spoke:

> there is a responsible Thinker and Actor working wherever a man works; . . . a true man belongs to no other time or place, but is the centre of things. ["Self-Reliance"][5]

That was metaphysical ballast enough, but a transcendental humanism also asked for teleological design in both individual experience and the history of the race. In this way it paralleled, or, more likely, pointed to the romantic source it shared with, optimistic evolutionary theory and the social teleologies of naturalist politics, like that of Marx. In any case, Emerson's faith is the right context in which to study later developments. Ironically, he lays a basis in these words for the harsher confidence or stoic passivity of naturalist fatalism:

> All things are moral. The soul which within us is a sentiment, outside of us is a law . . . . Justice is not postponed. A perfect

equity adjusts its balance in all parts of life . . . . Every secret is
told, every crime is punished, every virtue rewarded, every
wrong redressed in silence and certainty. ["Compensation," *ECW*
2:102]

Dreiser was able to express with even greater simplicity his sharp
reversal of the Emersonian faith—the faith that characterized
romantic naturalism. The reversal was easier than it seemed; it
required in some respects only the removal of the Emersonian
stress on "intelligence" and "spirit." (One is inevitably reminded
here of Marx's inversion of Hegel.) Emerson could say this:

We lie in the lap of immense intelligence, which makes us receivers of its truth and organs of its activity. [*ECW* 2:64]

Mere substitution of the word "force" for "intelligence" turns this
into a statement that Dreiser might have produced. But that would
have been later in his career, when he was imbued with quasi-
Marxist thought. In his earlier memoirs he reflects the pessimism,
or "wounded consciousness," of literary naturalism. He says that he
had learned to see

man's place in nature, his importance in the universe, this too,
too solid earth, man's very identity . . . as an infinitesimal speck of
energy or a "suspended equation" drawn or blown here and
there by larger forces in which he moved quite unconsciously as
an atom.[6]

If another analogy provided itself, beyond the atom specks of energy, it was that of the machine (though clearly a machine with no
pretensions to efficiency):

Man was a mechanism, undevised and uncreated, and a badly
and carelessly driven one at that.

In this way the premises of a naturalist ethos begin to assume
shape. If man is an energy, then the objective must be to control it,
presumably using energy to control energy. As Dreiser says, there
are always "larger forces." And if man is an inefficient mechanism,
then the purpose could be to "drive" it, but well and carefully. This
machine-like force has some capacity for response, but it is strictly
and reductively limited to "the hope for pleasure and the fear of
pain."

But finally, and most ambiguously, the problem remained, what
could be done *for* this creature-mechanism of hunger and fear?

All I could think of was that since nature would not or could not
do anything for man, he must, if he could, do something for

himself; and in this I saw no prospect, he being a product of these self-same accidental, indifferent and bitterly cruel forces.

In that last phrase Dreiser expresses a most important effect of the naturalist's sense of existential pathos, and at the same time he points to the important conditioning of a normative naturalism. As a standard of values it must reply to accident, indifference, or the unrelenting cruelty of nature, but it must do so not by defiance or by moving in the opposite, idealist, direction but rather by accepting the bleakness of reality's terms. For instance, if the god in history is cruel, that in itself may imply a direction that history must take to conform with that god's power or will. And if, according to Dreiser's remark, man would or could "do something for himself," his means might very well be simply a function of nature's cruelty. Thus, what might be described as depressed naturalism could be converted to its opposite, as Dreiser's own intellectual record reveals. The indifference of natural forces, the violence of man, might be directed toward the redemption of history; and naturalism, as Zola in fact originally declared its meaning, would then assume the character of a medical politics, a cruel science which heals.

In general, and in whichever direction it moved, the naturalist ethos emphasized harsh virtues, in more or less the terms Lovejoy used when he characterized it as "hard primitivism."[7] When nature is a teacher, it inculcates toughness, a competence for survival, sometimes a stoic gratification in accepting any ordeal as a test of one's mettle. Such imperatives have their source in simplified Darwinian precepts of the struggle for existence, the survival of the fittest. These could be used as the basis for self-magnification, for establishing the virtues of survivors and even the criteria for heroes.

The search for those virtues and for a standard of heroism is one theme of my discussion in this book. The procedure could be illustrated from the ideas of Nietzsche, and his work remains an indispensable reference point for any study of modern fiction. For instance, he illustrated the characteristic first effects of naturalist writing when he called for the ruthless unmasking of traditional idealizations, of whatever sort:

> [Beneath] all the deceptive junk and gold dust of unconscious human vanity; that even beneath such flattering colors and cosmetics the frightful basic text *homo natura*, must be recognized for what it is.[8]

This is the positive value, or stoic virtue, gained from naturalist shock: a dwelling on ugly truths in order to purge old lies.

> Life itself is essential assimilation, injury, violation of the foreign
> and the weaker, suppression, hardness, the forcing of one's own
> forms on something else, ingestion and—at least in its mildest
> form—exploitation.[9]

There is a whole history of modern political rationalization in
such words if we transfer both the aggressiveness and the griev-
ances of modern politics from the biological to the social context of
the terms "ingestion" and "exploitation."

But the hardness Nietzsche speaks of proves itself by its will to
accept the violence of nature and make it the basis of new values:

> I would rather perish than renounce this one thing; and truly,
> where there is perishing and the falling of leaves, behold, there
> life sacrifices itself—for the sake of power![10]

All death, all natural violence, is a celebration of power, and in fact
such "sacrifices" are direct revelations of the sacred mystery of
power. "What the people believe to be an evil betrays to me an
ancient will to power." From this we gain positive instruction.

> That is your entire will, you wisest men; it is a will to power; and
> that is so even when you talk of good and evil and of the assess-
> ment of values.[11]

There is a concise American version of Nietzsche's drama of
reduction and revelation in Stephen Crane's *The Red Badge of Courage*. In that book, war is the model of naturalist crisis, an explosion
of conflict toward which armies march like men in a "moving box."
The collision of armies, held together by the iron laws of tradition
and social emulation (as well as by the "deceptive junk" of "human
vanity") is like the collision of civilizations, breaking apart and then
forming again on whatever primary basis of pain, fear, courage,
and the instinct for survival that the battle crisis reveals. But beyond the realities of animal response, and in the driven rage and
despair of a struggle to the death, there is also a kind of ennoblement. This is not based on the conventions of military courage but
is a direct response to naturalist violence, as Crane tells the story. If
it is courage at all, it has been stripped of ideal ends and is simply
itself, "a sublime recklessness," a defiance that, since it "would have
shattered itself against the iron gates of the impossible," takes on
the note of sublimity.[12] The crisis of violence has provided a starting point as well as an apotheosis for measuring self-worth. What
has happened is that fear has become equated with weakness, courage with strength—both in an absolute sense. Possessing courage/
strength, one passes the test of nature, and in a deep irrational
response this is better than surviving. Crane's Henry Fleming, by

discovering his own power on the field of conflict, seems to dominate the naturalist fate that dictates entropy for every form of energy and death for every form of life. What Crane's soldiers learn in battle is that "they were not after all impotent . . . and they were men" (*RB* 94). What is represented here is not masculine pride in some narrow sense but a metaphysical pride, a minimal identity, a pride of existence. Implicitly, battle is an initiation, as if the ability to face death gives men the right to live. "He had been to touch the great death, and found that, after all, it was but the great death. He was a man" (*RB* 109). This crisis, which he found he could bear, brings him to the source of value-judgment: "He had been where there was red of blood and black of passion and he was escaped . . . . He saw that he was good" (*RB* 107).

As a parallel dramatic resolution, Crane also stresses that the battle crisis and the emulation demanded in the face of danger have forged a community that had not been there before or at least had not been so well tested and brought to high awareness. At the height of the battle, Crane writes that Fleming

> suddenly lost concern for himself . . . . He became not a man, but a member. He felt that something of which he was a part—a regiment, an army, a cause, or a country—was in a crisis. He was welded into a common personality which was dominated by a single desire. [*RB* 30]

I pursue this theme in a later discussion, but the clear implication is that war is the best metaphor for life, that the violence that most endangers life is the testing place as well as the birthplace of human values, ranging from proof of self-worth to appreciation of human solidarity.

It is apparent that Crane undercuts these neoprimitivist affirmations with irony, and recent arguments have emphasized the point by citing the stressed irony in earlier drafts of the novel that subsequently were altered, presumably at the publisher's urging.[13] The text that we have conveys mainly a sense of detachment, and, in obedience to the strict naturalist code, affirmations have no more place in it than outrage. Crane clearly believed he was reporting the actual rituals of manhood experienced in every war, occurring in every time and place. If he was a convinced ironist in that view of human conflict, his ironic vision gave him singularly sharp images of the male vitalist creed that was appearing in the contemporary work of Frank Norris and Jack London and would eventually appear in Hemingway's works, though these show that what is at issue for the later generation is not simply a primitivist entrance into nature's realm but a standard with which to oppose it. For in

Hemingway's writing the hero vitalistically affirms a strength and courage to match that of the bravest animals, but he transcends their virtues with his stoic bearing and complete consciousness. His genius is always marked by a proportionate pathos; for though he imposes a transient order upon naturalist conflict, the latter's terms are always deadly and inevitably fatal. Nevertheless, the pure value of order is involved in meeting this threat, and the heroism of risk-taking sport and brutal life demands and encourages art. In fact, art and sport suggest a deeper ethos, alive in a metaphysical confrontation and surviving on the verge of powerful chaos. Experience takes its shape there, as if, in Wallace Stevens' dominating phrase, death were indeed the only mother of beauty.

At the point where primordial violence touches the imagination and where, confirming Stevens with Yeats, "a terrible beauty is born," we may find the source of a greatly creative era of literature, dominated more, in the last analysis, by the spirit of Nietzsche than by Darwin or Marx. The poets—Eliot, Pound, Stevens, and Williams—reward us as much as the novelists in their imaginatively brilliant efforts to adapt, translate, or resist the premises of naturalist thought. But that study must be the work of another time and in a different frame. Here I am interested in the primary myth of naturalism and the ways in which the literature influenced by it submits to the thematic rule of conflict and power. From that center a large radius of effects can be anticipated, some of which I hope will be discerned clearly in the following pages.

2   The Naturalist Ethos

"Struggle is the father of all things"

From the beginning there was a morally reformist, specifically political, element in naturalist literary doctrines. Zola and the Goncourt brothers asserted that the naturalist novelists were like experimenters in medicine and physics. In seeking to understand nature in order to control it, they would join "the most useful and the most moral workers in the human workshop." As Zola put it:

> We are, in a word, experimental moralists, showing by experiment in what way a passion acts in a certain social condition. The day in which we gain control of the mechanism of this passion we can treat and reduce it.

And he went on to proclaim the high moral purpose of a scientific or naturalist politics:

> To be the master of good and evil, to regulate life, to regulate society, to solve in time all the problems of socialism, above all, to give justice a solid foundation.[1]

In a quieter voice Henry Adams was at the same time saying that education is essentially a Darwinian process of adaptation and a post-Darwinian strategy of seizing a degree of control over natural power. He and his brothers and sisters, he said, were trying to get an education in the mid-nineteenth century: "They knew no more than he what they wanted or what to do for it, but all were conscious that they would like to control power in some form; and the same thing could be said of an ant or an elephant."[2]

Actually, the fate of the ant or elephant was not the same, according to the Spencerians; the alternative to educated power was a good deal more simple and brutal:

> Under nature's law all alike are put on trial. If they are sufficiently complete to live, they *do* live, and it is well they should live. If they are not sufficiently complete to live, they die, and it is best they should die.[3]

Nature, in that sense, was self-moralizing, or had its own system of judgment and moved to its own equilibrium of order. Men might

13

submit to it or, more assertively, meet and rival nature on its own terms of power. This alternation between fatalism and strenuous exertion is the basis of the significant forms of naturalist politics in the nineteenth and twentieth centuries. Fascism, for example, was greeted by some intellectuals in Europe as a heroic expression of the human will—"the will of adaptation to reality" in the words of Pirandello.[4] As an artist himself, Pirandello, like Ezra Pound, saw in Mussolini an artist among politicians, capable of the great effort required for the task of ordering reality and giving life its form:

> Mussolini can only be blessed by somebody who has always felt the immanent tragedy of life, which, in order to exist in some way, requires a form, but which senses death in any form it assumes. For, since it is subject to continual change and motion, it feels itself imprisoned in any form. It rages and storms inside it and finally escapes from it. Mussolini has clearly shown that he is aware of this double and tragic necessity of movement and form, and hopes to conciliate the two. Form must not be a vain and empty idol. It must receive life, pulsating and quivering, so that it should be forever recreated and ready for the act which affirms itself and imposes itself on others.[5]

Hindsight bemuses us as we consider this juxtaposition of tragic form with the act that "imposes itself on others," that is, with force. The worship of form on this basis is revealed in the language that requires the sacrifice of life "pulsating and quivering" to keep the political form, the state, from being "a vain and empty idol." Further to demonstrate what truly must be called a rage for order, Pirandello goes far beyond the simple praise of realistic adaptation, even contradicting it by announcing that "reality only exists in man's power to create it."[6]

If force alone establishes truth, one must speak of a solipsism of power, for in this radical invitation to the will to act, the power that imposes itself on others turns everything else aside, whether it be an epistemological respect for things as they are or a faith in other and higher wills. The need to transcend chaos or, alternatively, submission to determinist fate lies behind these enthusiastic post-Nietzschean expressions. Gottfried Benn was another writer seduced by the temptations of fascism in its appearance as the master art of politics:

> The quality of the new youth is power. May it fulfill its destiny! May the tide of the race bear it over the years, houses, fields and trenches until the inextinguishable German form is joined by the new form, the form which is now dawning in us for the first time! Only then shall we finally realize the meaning of Nietzsche's

statement, as yet so obscure, about the sole justification of the world as an esthetic phenomenon.[7]

The esthetic of politics is the other face of naturalist politics, which was an effort to lead the struggle of forces to a resolution culminating in a new order. Youth, destiny, race, all collaborate in achieving the new form, whose highest expression is the state.

If this creed became fascism, it takes little effort to remember how, in Hitler's case, a pure and brutal violence overwhelmed its "esthetic" form. As a vulgar disciple of Darwin as well as Hegel and Nietzsche, Hitler put first his belief that "struggle is the father of all things":

> The idea of struggle is as old as life itself, for life is only pre- served because other living things perish through struggle . . . . Only through struggle has man raised himself above the animal world . . . . A *Weltanschauung* that denies the idea of struggle is contrary to nature and will lead a people that is guided by it to destruction.[8]

The seductive paradox here is typical: the brutal stuggle that conforms to nature also lifts man above the animal world. The more violent the struggle, then, the greater the redemptive pos- sibilities for transcending nature. Following natural law, the first task of naziism was to fulfill the right to bread, space, soil, and life; the ultimate task was to become "lords of the earth."[9] Hitler seemed to understand that the Marxists also accepted nature's law of con- flict, for he asserted that the chief difference between his creed and theirs was one of quality as opposed to quantity:

> The Jewish doctine of Marxism rejects the aristocratic principle of Nature and replaces the eternal privilege of power and strength by the mass of numbers and their dead weight.[10]

Race was the aristocratic imperative of Nature; weakness and dec- adence were bred out of the master race by its victories in war.

Marxist thought of course has immeasurably greater ethical complexity than Hitler's naturalist creed, but the parallel of major themes is important, the simplest and most basic linkage being that of the Darwinian struggle. Marx himself made this clear when, writing to Lassalle in 1861, he said that "Darwin's book is very important and serves me as a basis in natural science for the class struggle in history."[11] The analogy with Hitler's doctrine is a very general one and not meant to be reductive. Race was closer to vitalist imperatives than class, but economic competition would have little meaning in Marx's thought if it did not lead, for one side or the other, to the threat to survival. That in turn placed struggle in the foreground of human attention as both a political and meta-physical theme, but, more than that, it gave the partisans in the conflict the power to make moral judgments and issue moral commands.

The Right, the Real, and the Necessary

The precedent for seeking a basis for political theory in the natural sciences goes back to the eighteenth century, as Jacques Ellul has pointed out; for when the men of the democratic revolutions brought forward the view of society as "a species of nature," policy could claim to be scientific, and revolution itself could appear in history as "the moment of total, rational, and scientific policy."[12] Such a science of society could be deeply compromised, of course, by its link with the radical moral choices of a revolution. In actual effect, the imagination which conceives the apocalyptic "moment of total policy" is more religious than scientific. One would have to believe in this epiphanic vision, bow down to it as power, as Henry Adams did in half-mock worship of the Dynamo, or find it revealed, as D. H. Lawrence did when he said, "that which is and that which moves is twice godly."[13]

A "religion" of reality in that sense received its most ebullient expression in nineteenth-century thinkers influenced by Hegel and his nearest German disciples.[14] Carlyle and Emerson make an interesting pair in this respect, though so much of their thinking led to differing conclusions. In his essay "Fate," Emerson was as strenuous as Carlyle's heroes and his own in welcoming the opposition between circumstance and the human will, but he deeply protected his holistic faith by asserting, "All great force is real and elemental. There is no manufacturing a strong will," and, "Where power is shown in will, it must rest on the universal force" (*ECW* 6:28). With this sort of metaphysical guarantee, Emerson, like Carlyle, could grant absolute status to whatever comes of struggle:

> The day of days, the great day in the feast of life, is that in which the inward eye opens to the Unity in things, to the omnipresence of law:—sees that what is must be and ought to be, or is the best. This beatitude dips from on high down on us. [*ECW* 6:25]

Carlyle, who was less "inward" than Emerson, makes a clearer presentation of what we can call "action ethics," which follows the dictates of "god-like reality"—a phrase he marked for his own. The men who deserve hero worship are those who have demonstrated the will of the world in their actions:

A man is right and invincible, virtuous and on the road towards sure conquest, precisely, while he joins himself to the great deep Law of the World, in spite of all superficial laws, temporary appearances, profit-and-loss calculations; he is victorious while he co-operates with that great central Law, not victorious otherwise.[15]

His unequivocal statements make Carlyle perhaps the best representative of nineteenth-century moral determinism, more overt and explicit *as* a moralist than Marx. In a recent close study he is described as a forerunner of modern activist and fatalist politics—a Maoist before his time, so to speak.[16] The basis of this was Carlyle's willingness to allow power to be the agent of necessity and the arbiter of justice. He would grant that practical and ethical doubts assail human beings, but he said, "Doubt of any sort cannot be removed except by Action."[17] In other words, in history's terms, action is revelation, and successful action is history's accepted child. That faith was based on the Hegelian principle that the course of history

is the rational necessary course of the World-Spirit—that Spirit whose nature is always one and the same, but which unfolds this its one nature in the phenomena of the World's existence.[18]

If what is necessary is also just, revolutionary situations could be the high ground for testing historic right and wrong. Carlyle perceived this as the value of crises of violence, where "Force is not yet distinguished into Bidden and Forbidden" and where, therefore, as Philip Rosenberg has pointed out, success would be identical with justification.[19] A moral fatalism of this sort could generate opposed reactions. It might stimulate faith and the energy to prove that history's dictation of right blessed one's own side. But, on the other side, as the battle seemed to turn or as rhetoric convinced, the same fatalism could induce passivity in history's inevitable losers. In effect, the will to act politically then becomes not so much a desire to fulfill ethical purposes as a need to discover what these purposes are and to test their strength.

With this great justification of history, Hegel dominated the intellectual development that sought a metaphysical basis for politics, and it was Hegel who most impressively defined conflict as the motor of history. Marx transferred the dialectic from the Hegelian Idea or Spirit to material forces, from the struggle of nations to the struggle of classes; but Marx and Hegel both laid the essential common basis for deferring to history for the demonstration of which side is right in any conflict. Hegel's words were, "As to the proof, not I, but history at its completion, will produce it." Marx said, "History is the judge, the proletariat carries out the sentence." As Jacques Ellul has lucidly observed, that premise involves one of two attitudes, "either the suspension of judgment until the (final) rendering of proof, or the upholding of whatever in history seems assured of success, primarily power."[20]

Thus the outline of modern metapolitics can be studied most clearly in Marxism, with its rich accumulations of historical application and its deep roots in English economics and German philosophy. Under the inspiration of Marx, man becomes committed to his own "force" as the only alternative to remaining the plaything of mysterious natural and uncontrolled historical forces. If history is defined as struggle, then one must accept the power generated by it in order to master and transcend struggle. Power itself is generated by economic necessity, biological wants, and resources and is grasped by historic understanding. Isaiah Berlin's summary of this theme in Marxism is exactly centered on the way ultimate values are extracted from naturalist premises. The elements of a formula are evident: Men are members of the animal kingdom, the essence of history is the struggle of men to realize their full potentialities, and freedom is man's mastery of himself and those forces outside himself in nature and social process that would otherwise act on him arbitrarily. But action moves *toward* freedom; it is born not from it but from harsh necessity. Similarly, knowledge or contemplation wait upon action or the manifestion of "forces"; yet this dominance of action over thought, necessity over freedom, will lead ultimately to the unity of theory and practice, of "will, thought, and deed."[21]

The significance here is profound. Ultimate values are colored and determined by the drama of force meeting force, of action and counteraction. History is both fate and revelation; it is the judge, and what it brings is either redemption in freedom or destruction. At the same time, it teaches man the justice within his own strength, a justice made fierce by the opposing threats of class enslavement or historic extinction. In theoretical Marxism there is a sense in which ethics divides into the ethics of necessity and the ethics of freedom. The latter belongs to a different world, the one brought into being by the revolution, though history will of course instruct us for its form. The ethics of necessity, which is that of this world and the contemporary struggle, perfectly illustrates Santayana's point on normative naturalism, namely, that it seeks to find value in the energy which things embody. For Marx this faith was founded on the Hegelian premise that the real and the rational are equal to each other. The real, the rational, the necessary, and the right, all terms converged in the metaphysics of matter and force in Marx's translation of Hegelian terms. So holistic a system required the finishing touch of ethical grace. And this was the urgency of Hegel's teaching for both his right-wing and left-wing disciples, according to Berlin: "Nothing could be both evil and necessary, for whatever is real is justified because it is real."[22]

The large implications of a metapolitical system are evident here. In historic struggle each side engages in the lists of "necessity," expecting to be legitimized in the outcome. Practical Marxists might caution prudence and a strategic pluralism, but the implicit inspiring myth is one of force and fatalism, where force is given privilege in action and fatalism may be allowed to dominate judgment or moral response. Members of the various extremist cults of revolutionary violence do not apologize for violence because their faith in "action" and "reality" and "necessity" leads inevitably to force and because for them historic right has no proof but in victory.

Looking back on the corruption of Marxist metapolitics in the historic record, one can see how two options invited that corruption. The militant leaders could in the first place translate moral convictions into violence without inhibition, since force is the arbiter of historic judgment. On the other hand, they could translate force, even corrupt self-interest and power lust, into moral convictions, since there is no clear way of separating base motives from benign on the naturalist field of battle. Similarly, once in power, the party, having become the state, now has its certification in the political order rather than in struggle. Therefore it can judge the rational, the real, and the necessary for itself on a priori terms. This was what George Orwell, in *1984,* called "reality control": the party and state have complete freedom to decide what reality is, was, and will be, and they are aided in this by their presumption of having achieved exact rapport between history and policy, thought and reality, theory and practice.[23]

Marxism has been a singularly strong and successful political creed because of this claim to override contradictions and because of its ability to combine a powerful fatalism with an intense urge to do battle. The resemblance to religious crusades and jihads is obvious. I do not want to vulgarize or simplify Marxist doctrine here, but its redemptive determinism is most important for my purposes in understanding the dialectic of a naturalist ethos, where a fatalist view of power and conflict is converted to the use of a moral humanity. Marx believed in qualitative leaps or transitions in his dialectic of history, and the greatest leap of all is the one by which naturalism becomes humanism, that is, the one by which mankind is finally freed from nature. The details of the historic resolution of the cycles of class conflict were issues postponed for history itself to decide, but that resolution was in fact to be absolute, a transcendence of all the major contradictions of human experience and a solution to the "riddle of history." At least this was the faith of the younger Marx, speaking with full ardor in *The Economic and Philosophic Manuscripts of 1844,* where he described communism as the

> complete return of man to himself as a *social* (i.e., human) being—a return become conscious, and accomplished within the entire wealth of previous development. This communism, as fully developed naturalism, equals humanism, and as fully developed humanism equals naturalism; it is the *genuine* resolution of the conflict between man and nature and between man and man—the true resolution of the strife between existence and essence, between objectification and self-confirmation, between freedom and necessity, between the individual and the species. Communism is the riddle of history solved, and it knows itself to be this solution.[24]

The "riddle solved" was an ideal order but not one inspired by transcendental intervention, for the humanism remains naturalist at its source and in all its elements, and the problem was how to make a human order of the raw constituents of power and conflict, out of the material truths of human existence. Berlin points out how the transitions in the young Marx's thought show him turning from semiorthodox Hegelianism to a close reading of the English economists and the French socialist writers.[25] The economists, Malthus and Adam Smith, may have helped dispel "the mist of Hegelianism," but in part they confirmed Hegelian doctrine; for classical economics also made the proposal that a kind of order, or equilibrium, and prosperity as well, flowed automatically from economic conflict. In other words, a naturalist ethic might have been an effort to convert the Darwinian law of struggle to human use, but the socialist ethic was quite directly an effort to convert the capitalist law of competition.[26] The latter had been translated by Saint-Simon into the theory of classes and class conflict, and so the stage was set for Karl Marx as the supreme moralist of evolutionary conflict.

When it comes to moralizing naturalist truths, however, Marx has had at least one great rival in Freud. If one looks closely at Freud's summary review of social origins in *Civilization and Its Discontents,* the elements of modern naturalist culture and its potential for creating myths become awesomely clear. When Freud asked how civilization came about, he answered by citing first the dialectical struggle between Eros and Necessity, then the struggle between Eros and Thanatos, the death instinct. The greatest impediment to civilization, he said, was human aggression as an origi-

nal instinctual drive, because civilization is "a process in the service
of Eros, whose purpose is to combine single human individuals,
and after that families, then races, peoples and nations, into one
great unity, the unity of mankind." Necessity itself served that
unity, for the law of survival taught humans the advantage of
working in common. But neither Eros nor Necessity was sufficient
to guarantee civilization. Civilization was the organic result of a
struggle between the "natural aggressive instinct" and Eros, which
"shares world-dominion with it":

> And now, I think, the meaning of the evolution of civilization is
> no longer obscure to us. It must present the struggle between
> Eros and Death, between the instinct of life and the instinct of
> destruction, as it works itself out in the human species. This
> struggle is what all life essentially consists of, and the evolution of
> civilization may therefore be simply described as the struggle for
> life of the human species. And it is this battle of the giants that
> our nurse-maids try to appease with their lullaby about
> Heaven.[27]

Implicitly, Freud's stern science revives a primitive dualism, a
battle between giants called good and evil, but a battle which in any
case is enormously creative and therefore beneficial, since civilization itself grows from that struggle.[28] To capture the primitive note
in this, one should turn to D. H. Lawrence's adaptation of and dis-
sent from Freudian theory. Lawrence was one of the first to recognize that modern thought, even in its science, was beginning to re-
vive the old Titans and daimons. "The old religions," he reminds
us in *Apocalypse,* "were cults of vitality, potency, and power; we must
never forget it. Only the Hebrews were moral: and they only in
patches."[29]

For Lawrence, who had, one might say, the courage of Henry
Adams's convictions, power was indeed a god at the heart of things.
And what was most godlike was that which was most vital, thrust-
ing, and wild:

> From earliest times, man has been aware of a "power" or potency
> within him—and also outside him—which he has no ultimate
> control over . . . . Such are the sudden angers that spring upon us
> from within ourselves, passionate and terrible in passionate
> people, and the sudden accesses of violent desire, wild sexual
> desire, or violent hunger, or a great desire of any sort, even for
> sleep . . . . The Greeks would even have called it [this violence] a
> "god." . . . It is something beyond . . . yet within. . . . It is this
> which surges in us to make us move, to make us act, to make us
> bring forth something.[30]

There is very great imaginative simplicity in this, powerful in its
evocation of the myth latent in the secular teaching of both Freud

and Marx. The question was whether this god-in-life or god-in-history was to be with us or against us. That was how Lawrence put it, though he came to prefer "dragon" or "serpent" as the name for the naturalist daimon:

> man can have the serpent with him or against him. When his serpent is with him, he is almost divine. When his serpent is against him, he is stung and envenomed and defeated from within.[31]

To appease the serpent of power is the instrumental motive of a naturalist ethos. But appeasement could mean worship; for, in citing struggle as the first law of life, the new creed renewed the traditional drama of good and evil. In other words, to have traded the one God for many, and these for the Titans of power, was to have traveled backward in history without freeing man from the severest moral taskmasters.

Redemptive Violence and the Apocalypse

If force is the arbiter, if justice is the product of struggle, then we must look closely at the great historical turning points, when conflict has been decided one way or the other. The task now—reversing the traditional forms of moral universality—is to emphasize everything that particularizes identity, separates interest, and intensifies conflict. Each party to conflict, whether an individual, a class, or a nation, begins the test of historic right with heightened self-interest and self-assertion. Each must be what it is in the most direct and even brutal way, avoiding any appeal to a higher principle, whether peace, universal humanity, or a transcendent heaven. Again, the lesson was from Hegel. Berlin sums it up as it would be applied in Marxist theory, where every historic process is one of "necessary tension between incompatible forces each striving against the other"; this struggle, he says,

> is sometimes concealed and sometimes open, and can be traced in all provinces of conscious activity as the clash between so many rival physical, moral and intellectual attitudes and movements, each of which claims to provide total solutions and breeds new crises by its very onesidedness; it grows in strength and sharpness until it turns into an open conflict, which culminates in a final collision, the violence of which destroys all contenders.[32]

In this summary of the Hegelian political dialectic, Berlin stresses the enormous implications involved in the acceptance of "onesidedness" and the welcoming of, or at least a stoic submission to, the apocalypse. Revolution could become the center of a messianic cult of worship, but in any case the cataclysm was a gift from history. This was because progress, as Marx and Engels later affirmed, was not gradual; it occurred by leaps when quantitative change abruptly became qualitative:

> the [historic] tension, when it reaches the critical point, precipitates a cataclysm; the increase in quantity of intensity becomes a change of quality; rival forces working below the surface grow and accumulate and burst into the open; the impact of their encounter transforms the medium in which it occurs; as Engels was later to say, ice becomes water and water steam; slaves become serfs and serfs free men; all evolution ends in creative revolution in nature and society alike. In nature these forces are physical, chemical, biological: in society they are specifically economic and social.[33]

Rarely in human thought, apart perhaps from primitive rituals of sacrifice, had violent crisis been given so clear a redemptive function. This rationalization of violence received some of its most enthusiastic expressions in France, where, of course, the cult of revolution had a rich past. There was Proudhon, for instance, who said, "A revolution is an act of sovereign justice, in the order of moral facts, springing out of the necessity of things, and in consequence carrying with it its own justification."[34] In writing that, he might have been anticipating Sorel, who proposed that progress, which requires conflict, requires also the creation of "myths" to promote further conflict. A political myth is like a scientist's hypothesis, Sorel claimed; it does not have to be true before being tested in action, and its primary worth is its capacity to provoke action.[35] With approval he quoted Marx: "The man who draws up a programme for the future is a reactionary"; but, going further than Marx, he declared that, for historical effect, logical consistency and validity of prediction mean nothing.

> Marx wishes us to understand that the whole preparation of the proletariat depends solely on the organization of a stubborn, increasing, and passionate resistance to the present order of things.[36]

Thus it is Sorel, even more than Marx, who helps us understand the emotional and mythic color that belongs to the cult of political struggle. It is he who best saw the parallel with Christian apocalyptic thought and the role of redemptive violence in the historic success of that creed:

> These facts [of the history of Christian martyrdom] show us the way to a right understanding of the nature of lofty moral convictions; these never depend on reasoning or any education of

the individual will, but on a state of war . . . which finds expression in well-defined myths.[37]

Since history requires from men only a kind of acceleration in order to reach its climactic stages of conflict, Sorel felt free to advocate the dogmatic and irrational fanaticism that accompanied his "myths," and in adding to naturalist conflict the subjective attachment to "glory" he reversed the traditional relationship between idealizations and behavior. On the one hand, the high dream of glory would bring men to action, where everything waits to be demonstrated; but once there, in battle, "all other social considerations [are] subordinated to that of combat." Heroism had best be mindless; the shove given to history is what supports "glory." One forgets entirely, in a passage like the one below, that the embattled proletariat might be moved by reasons of justice and equality in their struggle. And in truth, on Sorel's terms, such "reasons" are only myths.

> The proletariat organizes itself for battle, separating itself distinctively from the other parts of the nation, and regarding itself as the great motive power of history, all other social considerations being subordinated to that of combat; it is very clearly conscious of the glory which will be attached to its historical role and of the heroism of its militant attitude; it longs for the final contest in which it will give proof of the whole measure of its valour.[38]

It could be Lawrence's serpent god who enjoins this heroism, who demands this sacrificial service. Believing in the religion of the real and in the cult of power, one may indeed long for "the final contest," but no transcendental vision of the future could be more mystifyingly absolute. At the same time, no faith could be more ruthlessly instrumental than this, since the greatest of sacrifices served only victory, and it was reactionary to count present cost as opposed to future reward. In a sense this is a pure ideology of war, based on unconditional surrender. For how can the loser extract conditions from the victor if the only issue acknowledged between them is power in battle?

The mystique of the historic cataclysm remained consistent, for it was expressed again, not so long ago, by Mao Tse-tung, writing in the Communist party journal *Hung Chi*. Urging unending struggle against the enemy, not relying on persuasion, he said

> Without destruction there will be no construction. Destruction means criticism and revolution.[39]

To conflate acts of destruction and construction in this way is of course to express absolute confidence in historic justification; but it also adds to the mystique of history the mystique of power. An apologist for fascism, writing in 1922, put this in his own way:

> Are we historians? Then we must give up sheer anti-Fascism. I do not see how one can oppose Fascism without renouncing every historical consideration. Fascism exists, it has won; for us historians this means that there are adequate reasons for its victory.[40]

As Julien Benda observed with great insight, the worship of sacred reality preserves the greatest respect for that which cannot be denied. But what cannot be denied—that is, abolished—by a sufficient force? The terrible Hegelian premise, "The history of the world is the justice of the world," leads inevitably to George Orwell's conclusion, which was, in the words of one commentator, that "the great phenomenon of this century is the rise of the power mode as an end in itself."[41]

Surveying the field, the student of these matters, despite a professional detachment, almost surrenders to his sense of fear. The fear arises from observing how many arguments and appeals converge to justify assertions of power and subservience to it. Since the judgment of history is relatively abstract and deferred, the ethic of political violence endorsed by Sorel, for instance, moved deeper for its rationalization than the logic of Hegel and Marx; it turned, one might say, from teleology to ontology. Hannah Arendt, discussing the terrorist apologetics of Frantz Fanon, observed traces in it of Bergson's *élan vital* as well as Sorel's more explicitly political advocacy. She summed up the combination this way:

> Have not men always equated death with "eternal rest," and does it not follow that where we have life we have struggle and unrest? Is not quiet a clear manifestation of lifelessness and decay? Is not violent action a prerogative of the young—those who presumably are fully alive? Therefore are not the praise of life and the praise of violence the same? Sorel, at any rate, thought along these lines sixty years ago.[42]

Praise of life and praise of violence are the same: this indeed may be the ultimate gospel of power. To say that aggression not only serves life but is its culminant expression seems to reverse the Freudian relationship of Eros and Thanatos, but it becomes a neo-Freudian paradox when the object of aggression is itself conceived as sick or dying. Often death itself is, after all, the only cure for the fatal deterioration of life. How much more blessed would be the cure performed by partial violence—the violence of the surgeon applied to an organ that is diseased—when some group or institution afflicts the body politic. Heavy witness might be collected for the medical language and imagery of modern politics, as Arendt suggests:

> The sicker the patient is supposed to be, the more likely that the surgeon will have the last word. Moreover, so long as we talk in non-political, biological terms, the glorifiers of violence can appeal to the undeniable fact that in the household of nature destruction and creation are but two sides of the natural process, so that collective action, quite apart from its inherent attraction, may appear as natural a prerequisite for the collective life of mankind as the struggle for survival and violent death for continuing life in the animal kingdom.[43]

The last sentence tells us almost all we have to know about the intellectual argument of naturalist politics. Survival is perhaps the chief issue to be settled. But the parallel obsession is with decadence. The revulsion aroused by images of decadence is deeper among artists and writers than among politicians, but it is in any case one of the strongest moralizing impulses of naturalist thought. The words of Antonin Artaud, the most explicit of the metaphysicians of conflict, would suggest that violence and decadence are linked by a law of nature. "In our present stage of degeneration it is through the skin that metaphysics must be made to reenter our minds."[44] The same dialectic links creation and destruction, birth and death, sickness and health. The last pair, for instance, embodies the clearest judgments one can expect from nature, and in the historic record they have been used to support the moral indignation directed at the decadent bourgeois empires of Europe in the early part of the century. Thus Thomas Mann welcomed the holocaust of 1914, expecting that it would finish

> a ghastly world, which is now over, or will be over once the great storm has passed! Was it not teeming with vermin of the spirit as with maggots? Was it not fermenting, reeking of the decay of civilization?[45]

Such expressions became familiar in the works of Ernst Jünger, Gottfried Benn, and others. Benedetto Croce, who, like Mann, later turned against his youthful political Nietzscheanism, supported the early fascist regime of Mussolini in part because it was pure of "democratic insipidities." But, interestingly, it was Marx he credited for this turn against the liberal tradition. Marx, he said, had returned him

> to the best traditions of Italian political science, thanks to the firm assertion of the principle of force, of struggle, of power, and the satirical and caustic opposition to the anti-historical and demo-

cratic insipidities of natural law doctrine—to the so-called ideals of 1789.[46]

Democratic banalities and insipidities were based, then, on the sentimental naturalism of the past. The debt Croce acknowledged to Marx, however, may have had the point of turning political thought not only from the soft tradition of 1789 but also from the grimmer, purer creed of naturalist struggle taught a hundred years later, which found its severest expression in Spencer and Nietzsche. One student of naturalist literature, Walter Rideout, in his study of American proletarian and radical fiction points out that in several cases—in Jack London, for example—writers were converted from Nietzsche to Marx, who provided them with a morally hopeful translation of the Nietzschean power struggle.[47] The theme is suggestive and perhaps can help to explain the wide and continuing ideological success of Marxism. The ethics of conflict cannot become a proper ethics unless conflict and its effects can be collectivized in the field; that is, unless it can both create and reward "human solidarity."[48] Similarly, power cannot become so singlemindedly a value unless it can be grasped by the powerless. C. Wright Mills gave strong if simplistic expression to this idea when he divided the world into two parts, the power elites and the powerless majority, the latter being people "driven by forces they can neither understand nor govern . . . [and] who feel that they are without purpose in an epoch in which they are without power."[49] On this ground the elite are more enviable than any of their material perquisites can explain. They glitter in their transcendence of the common lot—"the ordinary environments of ordinary men and women."[50] This in itself is an invitation to overthrow the power elite and replace them with a redemptive egalitarianism of power that would indeed be the solution of "the riddle of history."

The Role of the Avant-Garde

The modern avant-garde of art and literature defined itself in militancy, and cultural civil war became and remained its chief reason for being. The character of that war may have shifted from romantic underground resistance to victory over the establishment and the formation of a new avant-garde elite; still, the self-justifying theme could be called cultural subversion, as Lionel Trilling described it in his influential essay "On the Teaching of Modern Literature":

Any historian of the literature of the modern age will take virtually for granted the adversary intention, the actually subversive intention, that characterizes modern writing—he will perceive its clear purpose of detaching the reader from the habits of thought and feeling that the larger culture imposes; of giving him a ground and a vantage point from which to judge and condemn, and perhaps revise, the culture that produced him.[51]

This approach to modernism has several implications, not least among them the natural alliance between rebellious artists and revolutionary politics; but the aspect I would stress here is the high value placed on conflict as the strongest impulse in creativity. One later French critic committed to the avant-garde gave art the name of war:

> We no longer paint battles—we wage them . . . . The breaking of bonds is the very essence of poetry . . . . It is avant-garde art that . . . transfigures us and changes our conception of life.[52]

The most explicit call to this sort of battle was made by the Surrealists, though probably every art movement of the twentieth century was at least partly influenced by the cult of guerrilla war in the arts. André Breton, in the First Manifesto of the Surrealists (1924), proclaimed that the simplest Surrealist act was to fire blindly into a crowd as fast as one could pull the trigger. The crowd might represent the system of cretinous culture, a debased society; but whether the chief motive was to end that system remained obscure. Whatever the result, Surrealism, Breton said, expected nothing except from violence; it was an art of "total revolt, complete insubordination, of sabotage according to rule."[53]

Revolt in this language, addressed to art, becomes a metaphysical not a political concept; or perhaps it fuses the two so deeply that a merely instrumental or pragmatic politics can no longer be held in view. This idea is more clearly expressed by Antonin Artaud, who, elaborating on "cruelty," found it equivalent to "life":

> I employ the word "cruelty" in the sense of an appetite for life, a cosmic rigor and implacable necessity, in the gnostic sense of a living whirlwind that devours the darkness, in the sense of that pain apart from whose ineluctable necessity life could not continue; . . . I have therefore said "cruelty," as I might have said "life" or "necessity."[54]

This passage, with its orchestration of tones from Bergson, Nietzsche, and Hegel, is a fiercely characteristic statement of the early avant-garde; but "necessity" seems to be the word to conjure with here. Artaud was one of the few willing to go so far in conflating means and ends in the dialectic of conflict, but his words reveal the moral excitement that can inhabit the language and images of violence. The cruelty that life ordains, he said, will be bloody when necessary but not systematically so, [and it] can thus be identified with a kind of severe moral purity which is not afraid to pay life the price it must be paid.[55]

To be willing to pay life the price it demands is more than mere stoicism; it is a form of metaphysical martyrdom. Truth demands its saints, those willing to pass through the fires of contradiction and conflict in order to reach the limits of intelligible experience. As Breton said,

> We must proceed beyond our meaningless mental images . . . the insufficient, the absurd distinction between the beautiful and the ugly, the true and false, good and evil.[56]

These distinctions are vulgarized in conventional culture, are even the instruments of the bourgeois enemy; but apart from a political bitterness, the dialectic of conflict calls forth a religious hunger. Life's necessity and historic fate ordain violence, but its passion, in the old religious sense of the word, is aimed at the border between all action and thought, between power and value, between the life-force and its meaning. So Breton expressed himself:

> Everything tends to make us believe that there exists a certain point of the mind at which life and death, the real and the imagined, past and future . . . cease to be perceived as contradictions. Now, search as one may, one will never find another motivating force in the activities of the Surrealists than the hope of finding and fixing this point.[57]

This inversion of the religious passion must be felt in any effort to understand the modern cults of power and their invitations to extreme experience. It was a theme that Sartre connected to the political basis of his thought, during the French Resistance, by remembering the challenge of torture:

> obsessed as we were by these [Gestapo] tortures, a week did not go by that we did not ask ourselves: "Suppose I were tortured, what would I do?" And this question alone carries us to the very frontiers of ourselves and of the human.[58]

This is a most precise example of what Julien Benda called "the divinization of politics." By placing political martyrdom at the frontiers of meaning and giving semisacred significance to the torture chamber, Sartre was proposing an important variant on the myth of modern metapolitics. A sophisticated modern theologian helped make the same bridge between politics and religion by referring to the political struggles of Protestantism as an essential part of the fundamental religious confrontation. Paul Tillich produced an apt phrase, "the boundary-situation," to describe that struggle:

> we speak of the boundary-situation of man and assert that those struggles which at one time split a continent in two, so far from being struggles about backwoods problems, as Nietzsche says of Luther's efforts, were struggles bearing upon the human problem in general, the problem of the human boundary-situation.
>
> The human boundary-situation is encountered when human possibility reaches its limit, when human existence is confronted by an ultimate threat.[59]

Such challenges sum up what is demanded of men on the stage of struggle by the metaphysics of power and conflict.[60] That stage becomes a hero's pedestal, merited by creative acts in both art and politics. The same theater of conflict lifts men above the banality of cautious existence in bourgeois humanist culture. So the artist-politicians who first welcomed fascism saw it surrounded by an aura of metaphysical courage.[61] That was perhaps the climactic value in a range of temptations to experience crisis. Another was the simple masochism of fatalists, worshipers of the "necessary." Still another was the equating of all intensities of energy and beauty, which the Futurists proclaimed in their manifesto of 1909, a charter that clearly anticipated the more flamboyant claims of Mussolini's intellectual followers. The Futurists wished to exalt "the habit of energy and fearlessness" as well as "the love of danger"; of such things, they said, they would sing in their art. "We intend to exalt aggressive action . . . the racer's stride, the mortal leap, the punch and the slap." And if life is struggle, so, of course, is all beauty:

> Except in struggle, there is no more beauty. No work without an aggressive character can be a masterpiece. Poetry must be conceived as a violent attack on unknown forces, to reduce and prostrate them before man.[62]

Any ultimate intensity of experience can of course claim the attribute of beauty, particularly when it is united with the heroism of mastering "unknown forces," that is, achieving a rare order on difficult terms. "We already live in the absolute," Marinetti said, "because we have created eternal, omnipresent speed." Art, for the Futurists, was simply being brought up to date, made to confront the world defined by modern physics and created by modern technology. The paradoxical effect of this doctrine, as of naturalist politics, was to give credit to both defiance and submission, resistance and surrender, creation and destruction. The true absolute, of course, was not speed but power.

The bravado of café conversations is evident in these manifestos of the Futurists and Surrealists, but no one can dismiss the significance of their ideas or the vitality of the art movements themselves and their links with related and contrasting cults of modernism, including the Dadaists, the German Expressionists, and the Russian Constructivists. All these movements were joined, as Stephen Spender observed recently, in reviewing a valuable study of the Weimar artists, by the "now very visible pathos of the politics of art yearning toward the politics of revolution."[63]

But far more was involved than joining the "revolution of the imagination" with contemporary politics. The deeper need was felt in a longing not only for creativity but for order as well, and both were thought to have their genesis in power. We recall the energy and passion of Yeats in some of his greatest poetry. "A terrible beauty is born," he wrote in response to his own experience of political violence ("Easter, 1916"), as if tragic violence were a prescription for beauty. For him this violence was explicitly linked with the cycles of historic change, the great changes that stimulated every creative force by conjoining the destruction of an old order with the terrifying animal birth of the new, and it is Yeats who expresses better than any other poet the experience of passing through the dying twilight of the Victorian imagination to confront the actual "bestial floor," representing the drama of vitalist power to which, it seemed, all modern poetry would have to turn for both art and faith. The neo-Hegelian formula is reduced to clarity by Crazy Jane as she speaks to the Bishop:

> "Fair and foul are near of kin,
> And fair needs foul," I cried.

And this was the dialectic of beauty in her words, the price that must be paid for a created order:

> "But Love has pitched his mansion in
> The place of excrement;
> For nothing can be sole or whole
> That has not been rent."

To demonstrate briefly the similar dialectic of creativity and destruction in the work of Eliot requires an even greater degree of simplification. We know that Eliot's interest in the works of Frazer, Gilbert Murray, and Jessie Weston reflects the modern linkage of anthropological naturalism with religion. *The Waste Land* was first read as a major expression of the apocalyptic imagination, addressed to the disintegration of a world civilization. On one level it claims the purgative power that naturalist politicians and artists saw

in crises of violent destruction. But the metaphysical implications
are made clearer here by Eliot's use of classical anthropology,
which provided him with the powerful myth of the sacrificed and
dying God in whom he would believe, and which joined vitalist
magic with the spiritual hope of resurrection. But again, more is
involved here than the dramatic use of an explicit creed of redemption. Modern poets like Yeats and Eliot seemed to work as if
their images required the energy of destruction in order that form
might be a prize wrested by the controlling imagination from
scenes of violation or catastrophe. Violence dominates the dead,
dry land of the Fisher King, perhaps because the alternative was
dominance by the "hollow men"; the bang was better than the
whimper. Essentially, what was at stake was the ability to speak or
sing at all, as one learns from Eliot's use of the myth of Philomela,
whose birdsong flows from metamorphoses of the violence of remembered rape and cannibalism. The point is made clear by the
contrast between this and the passive sexual calisthenics, the yield-
ing to rape, on the part of the London typist. No nightingale sings
for *that* experience, only the hoarse gramophone.

Order requires disorder, peace requires war, health needs sickness: such was the dialectic that inspired many modern writers
whose experience and education had subjected them to the metaphysics of power and the covert ethics of naturalism. The extreme
case always gives the best illustration, and again the manic words of
Antonin Artaud speak most accurately to the center of this theme.
The theater, he says, should be like a plague, an epidemic, a holocaust, because that leads to a crisis that can be resolved only by
death or cure, by a choice between death or a violent purification.
He welcomes the crisis, the disease, the delirium that "exalts energy," for these lead to the "supreme equilibrium which cannot be
achieved without destruction." Destruction is indispensable to the
imagination, for not only does it cause masks to fall, revealing the
lies of the world, but "it shakes off the asphyxiating inertia of
matter." And finally, in a sentence that effectively links his thought
with the most sinister political temptations of the twentieth century,
Artaud says of destruction that, "in revealing to collectivities of
men their dark power, their hidden force, it invites them to take, in
the face of destiny, a superior and heroic attitude they would never
have assumed without it."[64]

It seems clear that the appeal of the modern avant-garde lay, one
way or another, in its call for a heroic attitude in the face of destiny,
against solid matter, and before the threat of natural chaos.
Perhaps the result would be sacrifice rather than victory, but the
apocalyptic drama was essential, as indicated by Artaud when he

banished all artists "dallying with forms," those who never make
the effort to reach that "fluctuating center which forms never
reach."[65] What the "center" is—life, truth, nature, God?—Artaud
hardly makes clear. What is certain is that reaching it requires the
collapse of all protective forms; art *is* the apocalypse, and artists
become "victims burnt at the stake, signaling through the flames."[66]

This is a way of certification, perhaps the only way to challenge
life to yield its meaning; for such dramatic sacrifices, even within
the fires of the apocalypse, might produce insight, beauty, order,
and wisdom because the metaphysical absolute was there, the energy which is the father of all things. In fact, the prize, in the pure
terms of art, could be a species of oedipal victory. That was the
vision of the hero-artist as expressed by Picasso, in language much
cooler than Artaud's, fragrant with the tangible paint and clay of
his achievement. In private conversations reported by Francoise
Gilot, his mistress, Picasso described his painting as an aggression
against the given world, even as an act of destruction:

> You see, for me a painting is a dramatic action in the course of
> which reality finds itself split apart. For me, that dramatic action
> takes precedence over all other considerations. The pure plastic
> act is only secondary as far as I'm concerned. What counts is the
> drama of that plastic act, the moment at which the universe
> comes out of itself and meets its own destruction.[67]

It is clear that for Picasso, at least, the drama was not one of
destruction only—of destruction for its own sake—because for him
art was master of both destruction and reconstruction. Perhaps the
latter was only latent, the beautiful promise, the power held by the
brush, which so much of modern art aimed chiefly to express.
Picasso was emphatic on exactly that point:

> Painting isn't a question of sensibility; it's a matter of seizing the
> power, taking over from nature, not expecting her to supply you
> with information and good advice . . . . Once the painter takes it
> into his head to arrive at an arbitrary determination of color, and
> uses one color that is not within nature's range but beyond it, he
> will choose, for all the rest, colors and relationships which burst
> out of nature's straitjacket. That's the way he asserts his freedom
> from nature. And that's what makes what he does interesting.[68]

In these words Picasso states more soberly and concisely what
Artaud meant by the "heroic attitude" of modern art. To think only
of modern fiction, one is reminded of the virtuosities of Joyce and
of a host of lesser artists who in one sense or another have tried to
seize power from nature. The contrast between the early literary
naturalists and the post-naturalist writers rests in the distinction

between surrendering to the power of nature, that is, accepting its terms of fatalist causality and external control, or challenging that power with the special combination of energy and intelligence available to the resurgent human imagination. The effects of challenging it range widely. First of all, it reveals to the collectivities of men "their dark power," their hidden force, as Artaud announced, and that was perhaps the most positive theme of naturalist culture in its move toward the "divinization of politics." But on the margins of that collective effort, the individual experience remained more creative, particularly for artists who could imagine the manic privacies of power or build subjective empires suspended on the string of consciousness. Nostalgia might be a resource, whether for irony or sentiment, reproducing, as it did for Henry Adams, images of order only to accent modern chaos, or presenting, as it did for Hemingway, images of violence meant to stress the heroism of a private grace or order. Heroism becomes its own cause for being—a pathos that begins with Stephen Crane's redundant announcement to the universe, "Sir, I exist," and ends with the stoic commendation of pain.

Beyond all this, however, and beyond the loss of the traditional normative orders of the imagination, something else survives, which I would locate chiefly in the work of Joyce, Faulkner, and Stevens. These I think were moralists of the future who salvaged judgment without sinking into the half-tragedies of pathos, defiance, or martyrdom. For clarity in this final emphasis one should go to Stevens's great essay, "The Noble Rider and the Sound of Words." Here his theme is the same as Picasso's: the gesture of the imagination in seizing power from nature. Stevens called that power the "pressure of reality," a force generated by modern science, technology, and politics, a force acting everywhere, but a "pressure great enough and prolonged enough to bring about the end of one era of the imagination and, if so, then great enough to bring about the beginning of another."[69] Stevens's own poetry illustrates the responses of the imagination, a counterpressure that seizes "reality" in new images of order. But that order is subordinate to the delight and freedom the artist feels in creating it. The dialogue of poetry is implicitly the dialogue of men, resisting order itself, or any authority of the finished thing, and, in Stevens's art, seeming to prefer the democratic uncertainty of its accomplishment. In the final words of his essay, Stevens seems to show how the imagination translates the commands of life and converts power into something other than the sinister counterforce of collectivities. It is the imagination itself that serves life, and it is imagination, whether ethical or esthetic, that deserves respect:

It is a violence from within that protects us from a violence without. It is the imagination pressing back against the pressure of reality. It seems, in the last analysis, to have something to do with our self-preservation; and that, no doubt, is why the expression of it, the sound of its words, helps us to live our lives.[70]

In themselves these words may not tell us what we want to know, but what they do urge is a return to the works of the imagination—works whose secrets have not yet been fully disclosed because what they suggest is a power differing from and eluding the grasp of a mechanist or vitalist power to which all other things can be reduced.

3 Henry Adams: The Metapolitics of Power and Order

The early American republic seemed blessed by a political creed based on natural law and affirmed by both rationalists and idealists, the school of Jefferson and that of Emerson. To the Enlightenment background of natural rights was added the inspiration of Romantic thought, both American and European. Certainly the writers of the American Romantic generation dramatized man's dependence on nature, and whether they expressed this, like Emerson, in a spirit of serene confidence or, like Melville, in tragic questioning, they forecast the shock to the democratic faith that naturalistic disillusionment in the later years of the nineteenth century would produce. For the issue then became whether freedom itself could continue to have meaning on nature's terms, against nature's superior force.

Democracy seemed, then, to require the strongest idealizations to support free choice. The work of Emerson, as Santayana once suggested, can be understood as an effort to replace static institutional ideals with the process of idealization itself.[1] The new democracy could not shelter itself under traditional forms or appeal to habit and obedience for support of its ideals. Idealization thus became naked to criticism.

So far as Emerson was concerned, however, the imagination was always the faculty of freedom, and reality itself was challenged if it seemed to oppose the intuitions of spirit. Nature was itself a part of spirit and came clothed in the garments of spirit. "The world is a temple whose walls are covered with emblems, pictures and commandments of the Deity."

Emerson could not conceive of a reality that did not carry meaning. "We are symbols and we inhabit symbols," he said. And if the world was, for some, still dark and brutish, that was due to a defect of consciousness: "Since everything in nature answers to a moral power, if any phenomenon remains brute and dark it is because the corresponding faculty in the observer is not active." A power determines events, but it acts through consciousness and choice and can be defined *only* through consciousness and choice. Idealization is thus supreme, and the human agents of idealization must understand, like poets, that in this world "the ideal shall be real to thee."[2] They are then properly free and members of a free community.

This was of course a radical idealism, and it invited a radical contradiction. If it should be decided that everything in nature answers to an *amoral* power, is beyond human idealizations—if nature exhibits the "colorless all-color of atheism," in Melville's phrase—that would demonstrate how insecure and even desperate the Emersonian faith was. Such a shift in awareness was treated on an epic scale by Melville, and it remains the source of the great appeal of his work to modern readers. In the simplest terms, Captain Ahab expresses a reversal of the Emersonian consciousness. He had come to know nature as violent force, whether man-making or man-breaking, and, retaining a Romantic sensibility, he had decided that its "right worship is defiance." The indignity of life in nature was what afflicted him most, much more than its physical terror; for terror could answer terror and violence meet violence: "I'd strike the sun if it insulted me." Pride seemed to be the only value left in a world of endless war, and for Ahab it became concentrated in a suicidal gesture of defiance and courage. Indeed, the power in nature was a barbaric god who left to man a strictly limited choice between heroic or ignoble destruction. In that choice was a warranty or guide for all behavior. If power is the language between man and nature, then Captain Ahab forecast a modern political naturalism by making it the language between men: "He would be democrat to all above; look, how he lords it over all below," Starbuck observes bitterly.[3] In appreciating the power in the whale, Ahab came to accept and aggrandize the power within himself. He created himself in nature's image, reversing what Melville would say of Emerson, that he created nature in the image of a quiet corner of New England.

The contrast provided by the benign prophet of Concord is the right context for understanding not only the towering symbolic figure of Melville's text but the deepest preoccupations of modern literary and political naturalism. In the tradition that makes the most striking break with Emersonian idealism, the obsession with nature's power and with naturalist process still dominates the imagination: Henry Adams liked to say in his ironic appreciations of his scientific and technological culture that coal is a divine power, so is electricity, and so, even more significantly, are sex and race. The question he held forth, the one that fixes our attention, is whether we must worship these powers. How many ages it took for ethical spirits and esthetic graces to preside over the natural crises of human experience we don't know, but it is with some awe that one observes the atavism in modern naturalist thought, which brings the rawer daimons back—"rough beast[s]," "slouch[ing] towards Bethlehem to be born."

In the American background of naturalist thought, Henry Adams is the transitional figure, paradigmatic because of his strong memory of being educated both by his sober ancestor, John Adams, and by the Emersonian strain of a democratic ideology. But reason and good will aside, Adams's great-grandfather prided himself on his realism and even based his constitutional theory of the democratic state on the rivalries of power, as the other American Founders did also, indebted as they were to Montesquieu. The words of John Adams could not be more blunt:

> Power must be opposed to power, force to force, strength to strength, interest to interest, as well as reason to reason, eloquence to eloquence, and passion to passion.[4]

Strangely enough, Henry Adams's concept of power was less tough-minded than this, though it was more cynical. A representative man of his time, he was disillusioned by the facts of power and thought that the men of the past (despite the contradiction here quoted from his ancestor) had placed all their confidence in what he, Henry Adams, called "a priori ethical judgements," a confidence now betrayed by the discovered truths of physics, biology, and economics. In the view of power introduced by late nineteenth-century pessimism, power is ubiquitous, it inhabits many agencies, it is indifferent to human value judgments, and it is entirely at home with reductive human "interests." Surrounded by the evidence from nature—as for instance, the horrible death of his sister from lockjaw—and by the corrupt war of appetency in business and politics of the Grant era, Adams felt himself stripped of an effective moral will and so, he thought, of a relationship with the democratic ethos of his ancestors.

Adams was thus in the best position to exhibit the typical shock effect of naturalist writing, where, as Saul Bellow's Henderson later expressed it, "truth comes in blows." However, as if he would avoid all blows, Adams made an obvious point of avoiding action, whether in politics, business, or even the academy; thus he assumed his lifetime persona—that of a passive, spectatorial, ironic, and subtly, comprehensively, despairing man. The manner includes petulance, for, as an Adams, he was trained to participate in power and was thus deeply attracted to it, as is evidenced by his life in Washington and his inability to avoid the social circles of power. Such a man could not remain indifferent to the new world of power realities, despite his own failure, and he became a fascinated observer at the rites of power, both in the natural sciences and in politics. As such, he often made the characteristic response of a modern wounded sensibility, to which he added the covert bitterness that is so strong a motif in naturalist and postnaturalist writing.

Adams was also the classic literary naturalist in moving from Romantic injury and nostalgic lament to the virile compensations of stoicism and from that to the oracular teaching of naturalist truths. He seems to illustrate what Santayana observed, that it is impossible for the human mind to confront "the energy which things embody" without giving it a daimonic or divine existence. Adams expressed this directly when he said he felt a strong urge to go down on his knees to the Dynamo. Despite the ironic hyperbole, he meant this; for he indicated the same awe and respect for power when he wrote about his friend John Hay's success in the nationalist and imperialist maneuvers of his time. Adams made of himself a notorious example of failure to adapt to the law of conflict and power relationships, but in doing so he only emphasized an ulterior respect for success and a real attraction to the arena of conflict.

Of chief concern here, however, is the literary strategy he adopted for confronting, or enduring, the naturalist conversion of values. He discovered the Virgin of Chartres, in the first instance to provide a somewhat sentimental moral contrast with his own age of the Dynamo. But the moral and religious contrast was deceptive, for the Virgin's real power was also derived from nature. She had her origin in a line of sex goddesses and mother divinities, deities of earth and blood, that is to say, life deities, in contrast to the divinity expressed by a mechanical energy. The Virgin, as Adams wished to see her, was the generating force of a large and beautiful civilization. Her energy translated itself directly into ethical and esthetic values. Chartres, its spires and windows, the rule of life, chivalrous behavior, the code of religion, all had their support in the purely sexual meaning of the Virgin. Thus what Adams revealed is perhaps the major theme of naturalist culture, the rivalry between mechanist and vitalist power and the need to seize vitalist power and its symbols as the only alternative to the rule of merely physical energy. Vitalist power, for some of Adams's contemporaries, centered in the creative evolutionary process. Such post-Darwinian affirmations were foreign to Adams's temperament, but still he yearned for a more positive view of history than the laws of thermodynamics could provide. The past had been ruled successfully by the Virgin, even if the future, the ultimate fate of the planet itself, was to be determined by the bleak concept of entropy.

The story Adams tells of his intellectual life in the *Education* describes the emergence of nineteenth-century naturalist doctrine in conflict with the traditional democratic ethic of idealizations. It further reveals the effort to sublimate power realities or convert them to the signs of value. In these respects Adams is a most important figure for cultural study, for his writing illustrates the convergence of a literary and myth-making temperament with an effort to understand science and the meeting of both in the explicit or covert creeds of modern politics.

The Myth of Power

The largest paradox associated with Adams and other naturalist thinkers is the fact that, as thinkers, they contributed to an ideological myth that subordinated ideas to the action of historic and natural forces. This myth was essentially a popular metaphysics based on presumed scientific revelations, and, like all such metaphysical expressions, it suggested a guide for human behavior. But politics and history, drawn from Adams's own experience and background, were as much the source of his thinking as science, and it is an open question whether they did not influence his view of science even more than Lord Kelvin and the Second Law of Thermodynamics influenced his instruction to the teachers of history. In any case, the multiple interests of Adams's intellectual life, which must include art, architecture, and literature as well as politics, history, and science, were subjected to his profound instinct for intellectual order. The result was that he wrote a legend of history and a legend of science, perhaps a gospel, if so steadfast an ironist, a man who almost made disillusionment a basis for action, could be called a gospelmaker. Still, even disappointment and defeat are services of worship if the object of worship is power and naturalist fate.

To understand what Adams wanted to communicate in this yearning for unity in the midst of multiplicity one must return to his premises, or theorems, which he loved to recite. His first is this:

Man is a force; so is the sun; so is a mathematical point, though without dimensions or known existence.[5]

This has an attractive simplicity appropriate to any myth. If there was a story to tell of the human past and predictions to be made for the future, the theme of both could be reduced to the movement of a force through space and time. One could understand events by using that abstract blend of physics and economics that Adams called his "dynamic theory of history":

> A dynamic theory . . . begins by begging the question; it defines
> Progress as the development and economy of Forces. Further, it
> defines force as anything that does, or helps to do work. [*E* 474]

If this is history, then politics—and for that matter, ethics—
becomes similarly reductive. The metaphors of physics, which now
condition all of Adams's observations of the human scene, are
applied as metaphors of engineering. The measures of energy and
efficiency begin to stand for the measures of value. But Adams, as a
nineteenth-century determinist, has no illusion that force and its
measures of energy and efficiency are things that human agents
control:

> Man commonly begs the question again by taking it for granted
> that he captures the forces. A dynamic theory, assigning attrac-
> tive forces to opposing bodies in proportion to the law of mass,
> takes for granted that the forces of nature capture man. [*E* 474]

Force is mass, force is collective, force is historical. The individual is drowned in the species, and the species itself is only a fraction
of the sum of forces in nature. There is actually only one way that
"the feeble atom or molecule called man" can assert a form of
control, and that is by identifying with the whole of which he is a
part or by discovering "the movement of the forces [that] control
the progress of his mind."

What Adams, in a word, implicitly teaches is submission to force
in order to gain the residual power that comes from identifying
with a larger collective force. In this he was like other nineteenth-
century moralizing naturalists, some of whom chose the force of
the nation or the race, believing that the historic movement was in
their favor. Others, like the Marxists, could identify with a social
class and the revolutionary apocalypse, and these were of course
the most faithful of all believers in the ultimacy of power and the
fatalism of the historic process.

The *Education* has great resonance today because of Adams's
prophetic sensitivity to the politics of race, nation, class, and empire
and to the apocalyptic motifs of revolution and decadence. These
were harsh but plausible reflections from Adams's naturalist
premises, but standing over them, in the softest light, was his vision
of Chartres. For Adams, the Virgin was not really a refuge from
nature or a sentimental or spiritual alternative to it; rather, she
was nature incarnate as benevolent, not hostile, force. She was the
vitalist goddess in the series leading from Venus to the Virgin, and
she, too, in her most congenial form, asked submission to her
power. Biological process, as Adams saw it, had thus raised one
daimon to rule human history, and physics apparently was now

raising another. The question in Adams's mind was whether the modern god in the machine, the Dynamo, could do as much to satisfy human emotions and all physical and civilized needs.

The Dream of Order

Adams had a vocabulary to illustrate his obsessions; "power" was one stressed term, "education" was another, "order" was a third. These were out of the dictionary of naturalist thought, as were "success" and "failure." Adams was led to judge finally that an education is less than nothing if it does not lead to power, if it cannot shape the expression of energy in life. In effect, education had become a Darwinian term; it meant adaptation or maladaptation to whatever the actual forces of the world declared themselves to be. So, in a lifelong spirit of ruefulness, Adams pondered the failure of his own education, as in this passage:

> Not a Polish Jew fresh from Warsaw or Cracow—not a furtive Yacoob or Ysaac still reeking of the Ghetto, snarling a weird Yiddish to the officers of the customs—but had a keener instinct, an intenser energy, and a freer hand than he—American of Americans, with Heaven knew how many Puritans and Patriots behind him, and an education that had cost a civil war. [*E* 238]

Adams speaks here as the representative of a vanishing species contemplating the advent of the cruder races that will supplant him. Everything that had trained that son of "Puritans and Patriots," including a bloody civil war, seemed to handicap rather than help him in competition with a struggling "Ysaac." This was not only an expression of bitterness, though the language is fierce, but a declaration of priorities. Culture must defer to nature; established values must bend to new energies in the stage reached by his civilization. The real contrast in his mind was with the actual non-Yiddish rulers of the world at that time. An heir of the Adamses marked himself for failure when he saw President Grant come to power. He called Grant an "animal force," advantaged in its push to the top by sheer stupidity and the corruption of morals. It is a mistake to overstress the personal grievance in Adams's memoir of failure. The failure was a subject of philosophic consideration, for it was the failure of a dominant class and culture that were being outdistanced by "keener instincts," "intenser energies."

Politics was Adams's inheritance and his best teacher. At least it rivaled science when he came to formulate his power theory, for before he could consent to the dominance of the power conflict in history he had to deal with his original political education, which had taught him a value theory. "For numberless generations," he said, "his predecessors had viewed the world chiefly as a thing to be reformed" (*E* 7). In his own life, however, as he spent the first half of *The Education* in demonstrating, this political moralizing chiefly concealed or rationalized the actual "forces" that generated events. It was in this sense that he could say that his education had cost him a "civil war," for it was Civil War politics, both at home and in London, that had taught him this bitter lesson, his chief teachers being Palmerston, Gladstone, and Russell while he served as his father's aide in the American embassy.

Adams gave seven chapters of *The Education* to this five-year period of his life, and, significantly, they precede the chapter in which he discusses the impact of Darwinism on his mind. Maybe it was Darwin and not Gladstone who taught him most; but Gladstone was telling moral lies, and that was what interested him most at the time. The gentlemen who ruled England were deviously siding with the Confederacy, and it was a miracle how much their real motives were concealed from themselves and how much they were in fact ethically honorable men:

> As political education, this lesson was to be crucial; it would decide the law of life. All these gentlemen were superlatively honorable; if one could not believe them, Truth in politics might be ignored as a delusion. [*E* 159]

Adams was able, many years after the event, to read the memoirs of both Gladstone and Russell and see them confess confusion, ineptitude, and self-ignorance. But while Gladstone at the time could hold the sincere delusion that intervention would be an act of friendliness for Americans of both sides, Adams could observe how relentlessly the pressure of British interests pulled them to the side of the Confederacy and how determined were British maneuvers to end the war by splitting the Union. Only one thing put an end to them, and that was the turning of force in favor of the Union armies on the battlefield.

As a result, in spite of his own conviction that only one side in that war was right, Adams was forced to conclude that "the actual drama [of history] is a pointless puzzle, without even an intrigue" (*E* 157). However, it was a pointless puzzle only if one made ethical reasoning the basis of one's analysis and predictions. The story was quite simple when described as a power conflict, which was the way Adams came to see it. The more serious consequence for a man interested in politics and a believer in democracy was put in the form of a question: "Could one afford to trust human nature in politics?" The answer to this was short: "History said not" (*E* 150).

Adams's tormenting of these questions reveals both his readiness to be disillusioned and his will to force politics to declare either its moral purity or corruption. It was a search that would not leave the realm of power, nor would it desert the realm of ethics. It was inevitable that he would press hard on terms that made a bridge between power and value, terms like "order" and "unity," which became the attributes of successful civilizations, like that of the thirteenth century. At the very beginning of *The Education* he pronounced that all education is moral in the primary sense that it is a search for order. Thus he said, "Chaos was the law of Nature; Order was the dream of man" (*E* 451). And this was finally the way he had to see the problem of ethical value in human behavior: as a dream of order. Order was a term that accommodated itself to power, and finally it *was* power, translated and transformed by usefulness and meaning:

> From cradle to grave this problem of running order through chaos, direction through space, discipline through freedom, unity through multiplicity has always been, and must always be, the task of education, as it is the moral of religion, philosophy, science, art, politics, and economy. [*E* 12]

It is instructive to observe Adams drawing a parallel between freedom and chaos, using terms like unity and discipline to describe "the task of education," and speaking of the "moral" of religion, philosophy, science, and so forth, for we thus see him as a confirmed naturalist with strong ethical and esthetic needs who had come to view all values as threatened by chaos. Against "power" and the random conflicting forces making for "chaos," he had turned to "order" as the value subordinating all others.

The reader of Adams's work understands the force of these contrasts between chaos and order, power and value, in the larger context of nineteenth-century political naturalism. When he states in *The Education* that he was a Darwinian "for fun," the spectatorial entertainment seems to match his ironic wonder at the antics of the British Cabinet during the Civil War. Perhaps he thought that Darwin's principle of natural selection was a kind of dispensation that relieved men like himself from ethical responsibility. If nature was amoral, why should men be otherwise? But we know that his amusement in observing Palmerston, Russell, and Gladstone was superficial, or rather a mask over his obviously desperate concern for the Union cause in the bad early days of the war. Similarly, Darwinism and what went with it were anything but "fun" for him. His account becomes much more than a series of intellectual postures of that sort when he was forced, by the death of his sister in

Italy, in the spring of 1870, to confront the lessons of nature directly.

"The last lesson—the sum and term of education—began then," he wrote in *The Education*. Since he was only thirty-two at the time, he must have meant that this was the "last" lesson because, marked by death's finality, it led to the answer to all his questions. "He had never seen Nature—only her surface—the sugar-coating that she shows to youth" (*E* 287). The passage in which he describes his sister's death, in a chapter entitled "Chaos," is one of the most finely edged in all his writing. Using the background of the rich and sensuous Italian spring to add the bitterness of natural paradox to a judgment of life, he wrote, of his sister's death,

> Nature enjoyed it, played with it, the horror added to her charm, she liked the torture, and smothered her victim with caresses.

Authentic as Adams's sense of horror surely was, the melodramatic quality of this description of Nature at her work is part of the protest. "[His] first serious consciousness of Nature's gesture—her attitude towards life," he said, "took form then as a phantasm, a nightmare, an insanity of force."

> For the first time, the stage-scenery of the senses collapsed; the human mind felt itself stripped naked, vibrating in a void of shapeless energies, with resistless mass, colliding, crushing, wasting, and destroying what these same energies had created and labored from eternity to perfect. [*E* 288]

This helps us appreciate Adams's obsession with order. If blind force can have this effect, humanly controlled and well-applied power might seem godlike; and if education was the paramount matter to pursue throughout one's life, it was because it held the possibility of wresting both power and order from nature's "insanity of force."

As if his sister's death were to be his sign now, Adams turned from nature to history and used almost the same language in viewing the public affairs of Europe in that same year, 1870:

> Society became fantastic, a vision of pantomime with a mechanical motion; and its so-called thought merged in the mere sense of life. [*E* 288]

Human affairs could not be given a moral interpretation, not when his sister's death was so violent. The analogy was founded on an older metaphysics, now turned sour and hopeless. We read ourselves in nature; and what it reveals to the mind, it teaches to the will.

Adams, after his two great educational experiences—the war

diplomacy in London and his sister's death in the Italian spring—himself became a teacher, an assistant professor of medieval history at Harvard. What he had learned he would have to teach: "In essence incoherent and immoral, history had either to be taught as such—or falsified" (*E* 301). These were bleak alternatives, and as a professional pessimist Adams seemed to gratify himself with them. But his continuing thought and the later development of his own "dynamic theory" tell us rather what deep intellectual taskmasters those extremes of falsehood and incoherence were. Whatever his style of gloom, Adams really expected that determinist history would reveal its secret, just as he waited for science to produce an endless array of newly discovered laws of nature. In this, too, Adams was a man of his time, ready to offer all his intellectual respect to the oracle of history and to accept its governance.

Scientist-Priest and Artist-Politician

Recalling his childhood, in the early pages of *The Education,* Adams remembered himself as a "ten-year-old priest and politician." A defrocked priest and unmantled politician, one might say, in view of his actual life. However, "priest" was no chance reference but sprang from a self-awareness that reached a climax in his imaginative submission to the world of Abelard, Saint Bernard, and Saint Francis. His feeling for the Catholic Middle Ages was complex, and, as students have noted, it embodied a highly personal version of the actual nature of the period, which he saw as the most completely successful effort to create a religious civilization in history. Paradoxically, he was led to the twelfth-century Church by the emotions of a fallen-away Puritan of the best American descent. This conjunction he noted himself, though he did not pursue the theological contradiction, which of course meant little to a secularized Yankee of the nineteenth century.

> Nature had given to the boy Henry a character that, in any previous century, would have led him into the Church; he inherited dogma and *a priori* thought from the beginning of time; and he scarcely needed a violent reaction like anti-slavery politics to sweep him back into Puritanism with a violence as great as that of a religious war. [*E* 26]

It isn't necessary here to separate the nostalgia for medieval Catholicism and the longing for the theocratic unity of his ancestors. The two traditions more or less cohered in his mind, for both presented strong contrasts to the cultural chaos prevailing in the America of his time. Yet it is clear that the two most important images in his obsession with the French Middle Ages, the Virgin and the stained glass of Chartres, struck at the heart of his Puritan inheritance. Adams, in exile from his culture, was searching for a refuge, and the alienation he felt included his far-off seventeenth-century ancestors as well as the powermongers and moneychangers of nineteenth-century American capitalism. But power itself, and particularly the new powers released by science, held him in awe. The power of politicians might be contemptible, particularly if, like Gladstone, they failed to acknowledge or understand it; but from the authority of physics one might infer an omnipotent Calvinist deity, predetermining what was elected or damned in nature. That authority could not be conditioned by human appeal; it was beyond the human rationalizations of justice, and, accordingly, it was possible for Adams to think of the Dynamo as a god when he confronted it at the Great Exposition of 1900 in Paris. It is doubtful that Adams had really deep spiritual needs, but he did need a metaphysics of authority that he could oppose to the moral cynicism toward which his life, lived near the seats of human power, threatened to lead him. The Dynamo became a "symbol of infinity." There it was, "scarcely humming an audible warning to stand a hair's breadth further for respect of power—while it would not wake the baby lying close against its frame" (E 380).

A "respect of power." But Adams found more than respect in his quizzical examination of his own responses. Irony was his style, but irony could not conceal his point, which was to say that, if you would be religious, this you must worship:

> Before the end, one began to pray to it; inherited instinct taught the natural expression of man before silent and infinite force. Among the thousand symbols of ultimate energy, the dynamo was not so human as some, but it was the most expressive. [E 380]

Adams's search for analogies led him to the Christian Cross, which, considered in terms of its historical effects, was also an emanation of ultimate energy. Therefore he could say that "the nearest approach to the revolution of 1900 was that of 310, when Constantine set up the Cross" (E 383).

What he seemed to "respect" most in the new power was that it defeated ordinary understanding. Radium and X-rays (to which he was introduced at this time by Samuel P. Langley) were scientific mysteries beyond the Dynamo, inaccessible to him. It is perhaps to the credit of Adams's mind that he could not develop a simply reductive view of science; but his imaginative ability to clothe science in mystification led him to the deeper implications of a religion of power. Radium rays, he said, were "occult, supersensual, irrational; they were a revelation of mysterious energy like that of the Cross; they were what, in terms of mediaeval science, were called immediate modes of the divine substance" (*E* 383).

In part, this was a half-mocking response to the defeat of his effort to trace the poor deluded ethical will of historical man in historical culture, but everything in his "failed" education prepared him for this "revelation of mysterious energy" and for submission to it. A "sequence of force" was a way of accounting for both a personal and a historical breakdown, as becomes clear from these famous words, which climax *The Education:*

> Satisfied that the sequence of men led to nothing and that the sequence of their society could lead no further, while the mere sequence of time was artificial, and the sequence of thought was chaos, he turned at last to the sequence of force; and thus it happened that, after ten years' pursuit, he found himself lying in the Gallery of Machines at the Great Exposition of 1900, with his historical neck broken by the sudden irruption of forces totally new. [*E* 382]

The neck that is broken is the neck of historical culture: a sequence of men and a sequence of thought. But Adams goes on to say that "he would risk translating [radioactive] rays into faith," and that means that his project would be to restore culture on the basis of the new revelations. How far he went in this direction is a matter of considerable interest; we can assume that he guessed that the world would do that work in any case. His own positive contribution could be only small, given his temperamental conservatism and the cultural shock that he and his generation had suffered at the hands of science. But faith is first a matter of authority, and Adams did have the compulsion to believe in the reality of a force that was strong enough to break one's historical neck. His starting point was here. He couldn't see relations or degrees among forces or between forces and their consequences, like the relationship between the Cross and the Gothic cathedral; "he could see only an absolute *fiat* in electricity as in faith" (*E* 381).

In effect, power could be the name for God, and what God did to make men love him or obey him was secondary to his power in being. Adams respected the example of Constantine, for instance, who used the Cross as if it were "a train of artillery, which, to his mind, it was" (*E* 479). He even made the analogy between that resourceful emperor and a modern broker who merged all the significant social and economic forces of his own time into a single trust, "which he enormously over-capitalized, and forced on the market" (*E* 478). The range of power was complete; no authoritarian imagination could hope for more than the Christian Cross accomplished:

The symbol represented the sum of nature—the Energy of modern science—and society believed it to be as real as X-rays; perhaps it was! The emperors used it like gunpowder in politics; the physicians used it like rays in medicine; the dying clung to it as the quintessence of force, to protect them from the forces of evil on their road to the next life. [E 479]

This was what Adams meant when he said that power could be measured only by the force of its attraction on the human mind. But in perfect circularity the power of value-images like the Cross and the Virgin was made manifest in their effects. The mode of thought has its consequences, particularly for historians, political prophets, and ambitious messengers of the Zeitgeist, ready to invoke new and old symbols like the Cross. What were the signs and proofs of power? One was the existence of great empires, evident syntheses of great force. Others were great wars and revolutions—incidents that hint of the apocalypse and can thus reveal the god in history. To engage in the politics of crisis and violence was therefore one way to force submission to that god and to conform to his will.

This was a politics of the future, one that Adams could not quite imagine, even though the politics of his own time had taught him the irrelevance of moral judgments. Much of The Education is devoted to that lesson, as when he observed that the most gentlemanly and honorable politicians in Washington were the champions of both slavery and secession. This same moral confusion surrounded him later in London, where he heard Lincoln called a monster by such decent figures of that era of enlightened conscience as Thackeray and where Gladstone, the monument of English liberalism, plotted fervently against the Union.

In the midst of these conflicting moral judgments, Adams himself began to react with excitement and passion to power itself when victory in the war began to move toward the Northern side. Power in action contrasted favorably with the duplicity of moral opinion and with the disorder of leadership in the early years of the war: "Somewhere behind the chaos in Washington power was taking shape . . .; it was massed and guided as it had not been before" (E 169). To Adams this was a major experience.

Life could never know more than a single such climax. In that form, education reached its limits. As the first great blows began to fall, one curled up in bed in the silence of night, to listen with incredulous hope. As the huge masses struck, one after another, with the precision of machinery, the opposing mass, the world shivered. Such development of power was unknown. The magnificent resistance and the return shocks heightened the suspense. During the July days [of 1863] Londoners were stupid with unbelief. They were learning from the Yankees how to fight. [*E* 169]

If he recognized that power had become the final arbiter, his joy in it seems to have become separated from any end which it served. He calls it a "climax" of life; he dwells on the shock of the blows and their precision; and he calls the resistance "magnificent." He was young then, of course, and, inevitably, he envied some of his friends who were actually on the battlefields. For him it was some recompense that he was fighting with his father in the equally important battles of war diplomacy, and in the spring of 1863 he began to see the turning of the tide there, too:

> Very slowly, indeed, after two years of solitude, one began to feel the first faint flush of new and imperial life. One was twenty-five years old, and quite ready to assert it; some of one's friends were wearing stars on their collars; some had won stars of a more enduring kind. At moments one's breath came quick. One began to dream the sensation of wielding unmeasured power. [*E* 168–69]

This high point of his youth serves as a contrast to the almost public pursuit of "failure" during the rest of his life—a failure which, on examination, was really a self-imposed passivity. It seemed to him—and in this he represents the first of several modern intellectual generations—that there was a breach between knowledge and power that could not be closed. The leaders of his own time he could view with a kind of awed contempt. Their power was raw, Grant was an animal, and Theodore Roosevelt he called "pure act." He felt the opposite of contempt, but an equal awe, for heroes reaching for the unattainable heights of science: Sir Charles Lyell, who taught him Darwinian evolution and geology, and Lord Kelvin, who taught him physics.

That disjunction in his experience only heightened Adams's respect for latent power and stimulated his appreciation of success. Success was measured by the amount of human energy needed to master the "forces" that challenged mankind. History itself was a kind of race in which men, societies, civilizations, must run simply to stay even. The strain of such competition was extreme because men were not competing with men but with something else—a process, a power, in things and events. He said this of himself, forgetting for a moment his chosen role of spectator: "His single thought was to keep in front of the movement [of history], and, if necessary, lead it to chaos, but never fall behind" (*E* 403).

The real question, finally, and one never resolved by Adams, concerned the role of mind in a world of force. Though he said that mind is itself a power, "the subtlest of all known forces" (*E* 476), he was evidently uncertain about its effectiveness as a power among powers, at least in politics. In *Mont-Saint-Michel and Chartres* he was clear about the great capacities of mind in architecture, the art of glass, literature, and theological speculation. In *The Education* he was deeply respectful of the scientific mind, which pitted itself against the complexities of nature and even its possible chaos. But in the actual use of power in human affairs—in government, politics, and economics—Adams was obliged to give dominance to rawer forms of energy. Initially, this was the power of gold, but he lived finally in a period ruled by even cruder forms of energy. "From Hammerfest to Cherbourg on one shore of the ocean— from Halifax to Norfolk on the other—one great empire was ruled by one great emperor—Coal" (*E* 415). If not in coal or electricity, significant power was in weapons for fighting or tools for navigating: "The fiction that society educated itself, or aimed at a conscious purpose, was upset by the compass and gunpowder which dragged and drove Europe at will through frightful bogs of learning" (*E* 483).

What a relief, then, to study old architecture, the massing of great stones into towering beauty, where it was impossible to see anything but order growing out of power. The stones surely didn't arrange themselves; they were specifically subordinate to a human agency; and so art in Adams's mind became the counterweight to the implications of reductive naturalism, as it was for others who devoted themselves to the high cult of art through the first half of the twentieth century. The triumph of mind in art stood in contrast to its debasement in politics, and Adams's severe judgment of his contemporary democracy must be seen in this light. He could judge the politics of his time as "the effect of unlimited power on limited mind" (*E* 418). Of this, President Roosevelt was the best example, for he "showed the singular primitive quality that belongs to ultimate matter" (*E* 417).

To find the larger portrait that contrasts with Roosevelt, one must go to *Mont-Saint-Michel and Chartres*. That book renders Adams's own "supreme fiction," which imagined a political civilization based on the knowledge of the scientist, the shaping skill of the artist, and the faith of the priest. (It was "empire-building," we remember, which John Hay's work "set off with artistic skill" [*E* 363].) In this direction lay the only way to conclude his education. It is an implicit vision of a natural aristocracy that sprang from "ultimate matter" and could master it, and in this Adams came closest of all to a central inspiration of modern intellectual politics.[6]

Adams did not wish for a civilization that could produce another Chartres; he wanted a civilization that could repel chaos. Chaos appeared to be the truth of nature; but if order was the dream of man, it was still the only dream worth having. Insofar as politics is concerned, the myth of power has only one conclusion: it must be transformed into a myth of order. Such a myth is endlessly inclusive. The religious triumph at Chartres is translated into politics, and both become for Adams a triumph of art and of civilized manners. There is actually very little concern in his text with divinity except as it is reflected in the inspiration of the Virgin's artists in glass and stone or is expressed in courtly love and its poetry. That cult of love and art was more interesting to Adams than the love of God, and, one might say, more interesting to his Goddess, the Virgin.

Adams had loved to pay court to women himself, in mock self-abasement, and it suited him completely to find a Goddess who loved courting, who was fiercely jealous, and who punished young men who deserted her favor for that of any other lady. To understand this, we must again recall that her rival was the Dynamo. Could any machine be as high-minded and attractive as Mary?

> Even in anger Mary always remained a great lady, and in her ordinary relations of society her manners were exquisite.[7]

In heaven, Adams goes on to say, the manners of the inhabitants are almost as stately as those of Roland and Oliver.

All this is fairly whimsical, and it expresses a confessed dilettante's view of a highly organized civilization based on religion. Adams's more serious intention, however, is to regain not religion but an esthetic politics by which to rule the world. All of his writing in *Mont-Saint-Michel and Chartres* is directed to suggesting that the high symbols of religion are part of a grand artifice, which is both a play with reality as well as the expression of reality's greatest energies. It suited his needs perfectly to explore the conventions of courtly love and to find the Virgin's worship at the center of that formal ballet of the imagination. He could enjoy its frank artificiality, its human expressiveness, and at the same time give attention to the Virgin's metaphysical—that is, her vitalist—sexual authority for both love and art:

> Courteous love was avowedly a form of drama, but not the less a force of society. Illusion for illusion, courteous love . . . was as substantial as any other convention;—the balance of trade, the rights of man, or the Athanasian creed. In that sense the illusions alone were real; if the Middle Ages had reflected only what was practical, nothing would have survived for us. [*MSM* 247]

If, as Adams thought, all civilized conventions are forms of drama, expressions of art, they are free to be illusions as long as the force behind them and the effects they produce are real.

The more reductive the ground of reality, the more license given to fancy or the imagination: this might be the formula Adams prepared for himself. He combined the worship of art with faith in science, and in this he spoke for his time.

> The fact, then as now, was Power, or its equivalent in exchange, but Frenchmen, while struggling for the Power, expressed it in terms of Art. [*MSM* 247]

It was "Power" that ruled all antitheses, including that of science and art and also the more vivid antithesis of vulgar economics and the religious sublime. Adams explained carefully that he was talking about a thousand-million-dollar investment in the Virgin in thirteenth-century France:

> Expenditure like this rests invariably on an economic idea. Just as the French of the nineteenth century invested their surplus capital in a railway system in the belief that they would make money by it in this life, in the thirteenth they trusted their money to the Queen of Heaven because of their belief in her power to repay it with interest in the life to come. [*MSM* 101]

He goes on to say that the bourgeoisie who had invested all this wealth later felt cheated and that the resulting reaction—the religious wars, in which the bourgeoisie and peasants attempted to recover their property from the Church—prostrated France. It was true that the capital investors of the Middle Ages wanted to shorten the road to Heaven, whereas those of the nineteenth century wanted to shorten the road to Paris, with modern railroads. Matching one against the other, whose investment paid a better return?

> Illusion for illusion,—granting for the moment that Mary was an illusion—the Virgin Mother in this instance [in the windows of Chartres] repaid to her worshippers a larger return for their money than the capitalist has ever been able to get, at least in this world, from any other illusion of wealth which he has tried to make a source of pleasure and profit. [*MSM* 106]

One can make a choice in favor of stained-glass windows over railroad trains and stations, but what is the choice based on, with what confidence is it asserted? It may be a distinction between fine values and gross values, decorative pleasures and solid utilities, but the real effect is to transfer attention to the fecund mystery of power itself. The point is that Gothic windows achieve a lightness or transparency of value compared to the grosser value of getting to Paris in a short time. Neither is a major value, neither has durability beyond the waywardness of human need and human choice. The result is to treat all values reductively under the headings of "illusion," "pleasure," and "profit." Alternating between cynicism and sentiment, Adams thus reflected the deeper temperament that accompanies a modern dissociation of values. Values, whether those of good manners or high art, could be spun out to the limits of fantasy and intellectual self-indulgence so long as the realm of fact was securely occupied by measures of force and matter.

In that respect there was weight behind Adams's willingness to call himself a dilettante. But was this how whole civilizations, that of the nineteenth century and that of the thirteenth, were to be measured? Adams said in *The Education* that "all the steam in the world could not, like the Virgin, build Chartres," but he had no way of convincing himself that this was true (*E* 388). The Virgin's energy was now rivaled by the energy of machines and electricity and by exotic supersensual forces like the X-ray, electronics, and radium. He was willing to call the Virgin and the machine "two kingdoms of force which had nothing in common but attraction" (*E* 383). But in the end that was how you measured force: by intensity of effect, by power of attraction.

For many readers, not content with so narrow a reduction, it may be more plausible to say that Adams's work is based on a traditional moral conflict, described by Leo Marx as "the ancient war between the kingdom of love and the kingdom of power."[8] Agreeing with Marx in seeing the Virgin as an ideal of affective and humanist sentiment, one critic, Michael Colacurcio, called Adams a "fideist" in the American tradition that includes Jonathan Edwards, Emerson, Hawthorne, and William James. The old problem was always that of reconciling "two kingdoms," whether these were defined as the kingdoms of God and man, nature and society, or human nature and the machine. According to Colacurcio, Adams too, despite all his involvements with physical matter and energy and even sexual energy, wished to "urge the transcendent value of the 'heart.'"[9] Robert Spiller, in an authoritative essay, is as emphatic in stating that the division in Adams's mind implied a preference: "As the power of the Virgin is humanity on the level of divinity, so that of the dynamo is mechanism raised to the infinite."[10] But this distinction, like that made by Colacurcio, in its direction toward traditional American humanism, leads away from Adams's actual theme. To have human emotions "raised to the level of divinity" would be mere sentiment—a distant response to force and not the force itself. Chartres was for Adams more than a reflection of humanity or even the powers of humanity. There was a god there, though not the traditional God of medieval theology. The fact is that the Virgin more closely resembles the Dynamo than the human heart, if the latter is regarded as the seat of sentiment and conventional idealizations.

Robert Mane, who reviews these variant approaches to the most problematic issue in the study of Adams's work, is right to say that the distinctions that Colacurcio and Spiller make do not properly characterize Adams, who was not a humanist and could not have believed in a "religion of the heart."[11] But Mane, in his important study, does argue that Adams was a "fideist" of one kind, and again he is right to dismiss earlier notions, like that of Paul Elmer More, who called Adams a "sentimental nihilist," and the similar judgment of Yvor Winters, who called him a "hedonistic nihilist." Adams did have a faith, Mane says, but it was esthetic in its major impulse, a religion of art:

> Imagination was Adams' real "refuge"; therein is to be found the "unity" of *Mont-Saint-Michel and Chartres* without which there would be no "meaning." Instead of a sentimental nihilism, what we shall see is the triumphant affirmation of Art.[12]

This esthetic religion puts Adams squarely at the center of the modernist tradition (as does his closeness to nihilism), but it would clarify matters, I think, to see behind it, and supporting it, a darker and more forbidding worship, that of the cult of power. If there are affirmations in Adams, they are related to real sources of power and to successful systems—or established ways—of using power. A "system of using power" is perhaps an accurate way of defining what art meant to him. Art was a refinement, a complication, and finally an ordering of nature's creative energies. "Order" and "unity" were terms he valued more than "art"; that is evident in the writing of *The Education*. That for him the chief significance of Chartres itself was not what we normally call esthetic but lay rather in its power to symbolize an achieved harmony of action and faith is clear from this final expression of nostalgia:

> we rise from our knees now, we have finished our pilgrimage. We have done with Chartres . . .; we shall see it no more, and can safely leave the Virgin in her majesty . . . looking down from a deserted heaven, into an empty church, on a dead faith. [*MSM* 213]

This is not a speech addressed to a still-visible great art; it is a farewell to a dead world and the lost power that held it together.

Adams wanted to believe in the unity of the thirteenth century because he believed without any doubt whatsoever in the fact of modern disorder. His critique of modern civilization is a total criticism, based on emotional, moral, and esthetic needs. He admired a social unity more than the structural unity of a cathedral, and that in fact was what he *saw* in Chartres. The point is that Adams was not serving the specialized needs of the esthetic imagination or those of the ethical imagination. It was the metaphysical imagination that led him to Chartres; but since his metaphysics was keyed to power, his point of view turned toward an inclusive politics of order. It is a mistake to describe this vivid modern intelligence as one driven by nostalgia, for it was the future that preoccupied him, and what he predicted, in a remarkably clear vision, was a state and civilization dominated by totalist concepts of power and order.

Vitalist Power and the Goddess of Order

The Virgin, like Henry Adams, had no love for moneylenders, and, though he said that she was a thousand-million-dollar investment in thirteenth-century France, he could not be content with a mere economic explanation of her power. Going to heaven, even for a French bourgeois, could not really be equated with a profitable investment. In Adams's own civilization (and that of the Virgin was shaped in his mind as its antithesis), it was evident that the common pursuit was money and that money in turn was the universal medium of power. Therefore, all the things that money could buy might be reduced to the same value, for all were cursed by the same reductive symbol, which trivialized every article in the market of exchange, the most expensive along with the cheapest.

If power is always at the center of life, then money, in Adams's America, was certainly power. This was the degrading reduction that Adams most disliked in the trend of his own thought; but the Virgin, if not her God, offered an alternative. The reductive source of her power might repel some nineteenth-century minds, but when the crude expressions of economic reduction were faced, it might seem a better choice to engage in vitalism as a way of approaching the power that generated society and directed human history. Adams himself, in his ruminations on the future, was attracted to the vitalist politics of race. But the cult of the Virgin offered a deeper natural force than race to compete with the principles of political economy. Writing when he did, Adams could have read the early volumes of *The Golden Bough* and so have been affected by the revelations of Frazer's vitalist anthropology. We know that he was deeply impressed by Bergson's thought as marking the intellectual trend of the future.[13] In any case, he was ready to appreciate the naturalist genealogy of the gods, and particularly the ancestry of the sex goddess:

> The scientific mind is atrophied, and suffers under inherited cerebral weakness, when it comes in contact with the eternal woman—Astarte, Isis, Demeter, Aphrodite, and the last and greatest deity of all, the Virgin . . . . The study of Our Lady, as shown by the art of Chartres, leads directly back to Eve, and lays bare the whole subject of sex. [*MSM* 215][14]

This was very daring, if not crudely blasphemous, and so it was easier to suggest that "the best starting-point for study of the Virgin would be a practical acquaintance with bees, and especially with queen bees" (*MSM* 215). Euphemism was necessary to a man like Adams in dealing with sex, a theme of great violence in every nineteenth-century mind. His way of treating the Venus-Virgin by dwelling on stone and glass images in the old cathedrals was characteristic. It was a case of the genteel tradition rebelling only mildly against itself in the oversublimated mind of a Boston American of the post-Victorian era. The safe distance he maintained from grossness is evidenced by his choosing Saint Francis as another hero of his vitalist romance. Saint Francis, Adams said, "was elementary nature itself . . .; he was Greek in his joy of life" (*MSM* 375).

There was nothing vulgar about Saint Francis, and, after all, the choices were limited in Adams's own time. He could deal with a straightforward primitivism or seek the attenuated values of the higher estheticism, in the style of the end of the century. Adams, however, made a lucky find in the Virgin of Chartres, for she was the mistress of a great art, and there was a sensational outpouring of esthetic sensibility in her service; at the same time, she embodied the natural power most certain to be coterminous with life itself. He wanted Unity, and he found it, with emphasis, at Chartres.

Adams's need to desublimate nature—that is, to reach directly to its actual source of power—puts him truly in the avant-garde of twentieth-century writing and thought. The imaginative extremes in his worship of power arose from his own sense of powerlessness, a quality inherent no doubt in the psychic equipment of most of the creative contributors to the modern culture of power. Nietzsche, a near invalid for most of his life before his final collapse, felt the same need to desublimate nature, but Adams was a typical American case, as he said himself. The theme is dramatically present also in the poetry of Eliot, another refugee from the "genteel tradition." Prufrock and Gerontion live in the dead end of stale sublimations, brought conclusively to view in *The Waste Land*, where the Fisher King myth links vitalist (or sexual) impotence with the failure of religious belief. In a more exact parallel with Adams, Eliot imagined incarnations of sexual love and tragedy moving toward the transcendent (with the model of Dante's Beatrice strongly in mind), to be redeemed by the actual Rose of the Virgin.

Like Adams, Eliot perhaps felt that he could purge his own demons by connecting divinity with the primary revelations of sexual energy. For both writers, natural power threatened deadly chaos unless it could produce redemption from within itself. For Adams, woman is a triumph of nature because she combines a pure animal energy with the force that creates family and social order. A somewhat overcivilized gentleman thus gave himself license to believe that the primary energy in sex arises in women and that men are, so to speak, only agents of response. ("If it were worth while to argue a paradox, one might maintain that Nature regards the female as the essential, the male as the superfluity of her world" [*MSM* 215].) Maternity was not a separate issue in his mind; in the traditional manner, it purified and uplifted sex. The Virgin perhaps could be the nineteenth century's ideal of the married woman and mother, disregarding for the moment the actual complexities in the medieval view of her. She had all the attributes of the natural woman but still was virginal, still pure. She arose from life and yet transcended it; no one could call her the prisoner of her body. It is a fine irony that she should therefore become the right symbol for a sophisticated son of the Puritans.

Adams, however, did try, in his own way, to do justice to the actual power of sex. He felt that something was wrong with his world because America and northern Europe did not know the Virgin, not because their culture lacked a symbol of purity but because it lacked a transcendent symbol of sex. His civilization, industrial and scientifically advanced, had unleashed unbelievable power in the world, but it was power of the wrong sort. He therefore tried to imagine a power that generated order not as a check on its own strength but as an expression of it. Thus he found his theme. He stated it in a letter written before he wrote the book inspired by the Virgin:

> I admit that the American woman is a failure; that she has held nothing together, neither State nor Church, nor Society nor Family.... Our fascinating old 12th-century friends had a job that could be handled.... America has nearly a hundred million people running at least five-and-twenty million horse-power equivalent to the power of the whole animal world since Eve. It worries me to see our women run away from the job.[15]

In sum, one can find in Adams's cult of the Virgin a full range of responses reflecting the great exchange that took place between mechanist and vitalist thought, both in his time and later. In the context of pure mechanism, the choice of sexual power for allegiance and cultivation was comprehensible. In the context of business and politics—the modern counterpart of the male vitalism of hunting and fighting societies—the choice of godlike femininity was even more understandable, at least for Adams, who accepted a lifelong alienation from the realms of male power in his America.

More significantly, the Virgin provided a way to resist the rule enclosing men on all sides in historic process, biological fate, and the abstract equations of economics and physics. In Adams's view, the Virgin's power was as subversive as it was authoritative, and this complexity he could justify as part of vitalism, or nature's religion. The Virgin challenged every rational order, even the Church, because she governed through human instincts and feelings. The Church, Adams says, could not coherently express Mariolatry as doctrine, and yet the Church and all its doctrines "were at the mercy of Mary's will." Even the devils were exasperated, he delights in saying, by Mary's exercise of a wholly arbitrary and illegitimate power (*MSM* 304). Mary became, then, the intercessor for mankind, a kind of female Prometheus, championing the human interest against the power that could alternately appear as brutal chaos or as a repressively rational order:

> Mary concentrated in herself the whole rebellion of man against fate; the whole protest against divine law; the whole contempt for human law as its outcome; the whole unutterable fury of human nature beating itself against the walls of its prison-house, and suddenly seized by a hope that in the Virgin man had found a door of escape. She was above law; she took feminine pleasure in turning hell into an ornament; she delighted in trampling on every social distinction in this world and the next. She knew that the universe was unintelligible to her, on any theory of morals, as it was to her worshippers, and she felt, like them, no sure conviction that it was any more intelligible to the Creator of it. [*MSM* 307]

Needless to say, this is not the theory of any scholar of the medieval Church. Nor is it the heresy of a believer. The passage is comprehensible only in terms of a nineteenth-century vision of nature's newly revealed god of ambiguous justice, ruthless in awarding punishment, perhaps gratuitous in his rewards, and in any case deaf to human appeal. Such a god could stir an oedipal response and lead plausibly to the "female vitalism" of the Virgin cult. We must remember that the Virgin was Catholic, while the religion of Adams's Calvinist ancestors was what he would call a male religion. In his own time, Darwin, Marx, and his brother

Brooks Adams all seemed to preach a form of divine election and damnation in historic struggle. In contrast, Mary offered a special forgiveness for weakness and for breach of the law:

> If the Trinity was in its essence Unity, the Mother alone would represent whatever was not Unity; whatever was irregular, exceptional, outlawed; and this was the whole human race. [*MSM* 290]

In this Mother's home, the cathedral, "one sees her personal presence on every side. Any one can feel it who will only consent to feel like a child" (*MSM* 193). If one played at the feet of the Mother, there was license to be a child.

To feel like a child, however, was to know how to accept and submit to absolute authority. In the end, whatever Adams has had to say about love or sympathy, he returns to an image of unlimited power. He describes the Virgin as seen in the outer panel of glass in the sanctuary:

> in the act of seating herself, we should see her pause a moment to look down with love and sympathy on us—her people—who pack the enormous hall, and throng far out beyond the open portals; while, an instant later, she glances up to see that her great lords, spiritual and temporal, the advisers of her judgement, the supports of her authority, the agents of her will, shall be in place; . . . all of them ready at a sign to carry out a sentence of judgement or an errand of mercy; to touch with the sceptre or to strike with the sword; and never err. [*MSM* 198]

This perfection of authority was ultimately what Adams wanted from imaginative belief: everything in its place and "the agents of her will." The vision is one of reconciliation between value and power, with the words "love," "sympathy," and "mercy" fused with "sentence of judgement" and "strike with the sword." Adams needed to make power sympathetic in the image of the Divine Mother, but he felt an equally strong need to believe that she could "never err." Even the spirit of unreason, even the transgressor, acknowledged her power. How much wider could omnipotence be stretched? And since Adams was never in the least a mystic, or even a religious person, his vision suggests his deep need to conciliate power and submit to it.

This is the ground on which to understand Adams's nostalgic journey to the Middle Ages and the shrines of the Virgin. She was a force in nature, a manifestation of the ageless sex goddess and maternal power which had been recognized by the highest Christian divinity. And so she ruled imperially, the greatest of queens, whose power was supreme because she was able to arouse a faith in proportion to her vitalist force and truth. Adams dealt frankly with sublimations, and, when he said "love is law," he meant that it leads to the ordering of life. Religious inspiration itself seemed finally to him an instrument of high politics; for what he longed for was not a personal union with God but the harmony of a civilization like that of the Romans or medieval Normans.

Explicitly, Adams wanted to say that the Virgin was the greatest political force that had ever appeared on earth. She did not exist as a mere supplementary source of tenderness or mercy alongside the omnipotent Son and Father, for she ruled, and she exacted prompt and willing obedience from king and bishop. She protected her friends and punished her enemies, thus proving her authority real, not confined to working through the inner religious conscience. She was indeed Roman and carried no aura of the manger or the worship of shepherds on the Judean hills. Adams was impressed by the fact that her authority arose from her recognition by Constantine's mother, the Empress Helena, as the result of her pilgrimage to Jerusalem in 326. In other words, the Virgin's royal heritage was clear; she was genuinely of the Roman empire and expressed the principle of empire:

> She was not a Western, feudal queen, nor was her Son a feudal king; she typified an authority which the people wanted, and the fiefs feared; the Pax Romana; the omnipotence of God in government. In all Europe, at that time, there was no power able to enforce justice or to maintain order, and no symbol of such a power except Christ and his Mother and the Imperial Crown. [*MSM* 79–80]

There was nothing to challenge the legitimacy of her rule when she, her cathedrals, and all her civilization so completely expressed "the thought of infinite energy." The god in the coalpit, the Dynamo, was now her metaphysical rival, but it could hardly do as much to reward respect for "infinite energy." A "constitution" for the world based on metaphysical authority was what Adams wanted, expressing himself in terms of his family's political tradition. It seems to have been the fate of the Adamses to act as the questioners of the democratic faith and to be most alert to its intellectual and historic vulnerability, even to the point of the defeatism expressed by Henry and Brooks, the last of their line. Far from being the eccentric and tired progeny of a rich tradition, as it was once thought, it seems clearer today that their minds were in the vanguard of the nineteenth-century battle for the survival of liberal philosophy and that in Henry Adams's thinking in particular there can be found a turning point in the cultural and intellectual history of democracy. Post-Darwinian biology and modern physics taught him the abstractions of power and species. In that vein he was forced to think of the "animal"—"not a concept"—that rules history, whether in the form of sex, or race, or nation, or class, or party. Biology and physics also taught conflict, raised to a determinant principle of the life-process, and entropy, which brought every process into deathlike stasis. These terms threatened anarchy in life and politics, and so Adams was bent on forcing science to yield abstractions for energy that supported unity, not multiplicity; order, not chaos.

The trouble with democracy, for instance, was that it was like an unfinished scientific experiment in a field of energy. It revealed power, all right, but where was its unity, its system of law? In the state, there were aggregations of energy called party, class, group, or simply forceful individuals like Roosevelt, who exemplified what Adams called the animal force of leaders. But these quanta of energy could not make their own law, nor could they will their unity into being. Perhaps in the time of his ancestors, by a fiction of the a priori moral imagination, they could; but now these units were fragments of energy, drifting and colliding and desperately in need of an ordering principle, like gravity or radiation, by which they could cohere.

The democracy that Adams studied all his life with ambivalent reactions was precisely what he called "multiplistic," and to him this term came to mean decadence and the entropic loss of cultural energy. If the men of science and religion were trying to bridge multiplicity, then the effort of democratic politicians was wrong and moved in the opposite direction, or so it seemed to Adams, who had little temperamental sympathy for compromise or the crude forms of conciliation in democratic politics. It was also true that Adams had little of the actual temperament of the scientist. Thus, when the scientists of his time reported a world of phenomena that seemed to disappear into chaos, having no unifying law or coherent relationship, he felt a despair that most of them did not feel.

Science gave no assurance, but science had raised the threat to the liberal philosophy of his ancestors, a threat that Adams's life and work so clearly illustrate. The monolithic and reductive language of power had led to a moral crisis. It was evident that Adams could not bring together or synthesize power and value, power and justice, power and liberty. Neither did he know how they could exist apart. The virtuosity of naturalist politics (and the debate in Adams's mind provides a clear outline of that form of metapolitics) was to demonstrate the historic direction of conflict toward order, or equilibrium, even if the forces in conflict were more unruly than those subdued by the maternal and sexual attraction of the Virgin. The racial and economic-class politics of his own time were keenly understood by Adams, and he prophesied with ominous clarity the politics of ours.

The naturalist bias in political thought must be evaluated in this context. Power was the name for what happened in history, for the often mysterious effective causes of events. "Value" was the name of the language men used for masking their power, or it was the name for their disappointments, or at best it was the name for their dreams. That melancholy conclusion dominates the pages of *The Education* and Adams's letters. But significantly, as he said himself, he found comfort in deserting a priori idealizations for stoic a posteriori affirmations. That is to say, it is futile to try to run ahead of history, but one may catch up from behind. In effect, one comes to terms with real causes, real power. Empire and world order, an implicit doctrine of race, a vitalist metaphysics of sex—these finally defined Adams's beliefs, and they were graced by historic illustration in the sovereignty of the Virgin, who inspired religion and art, law and the state, war and peace. The alternatives to her rule—or to rule by powers like her—were entropic decadence, disorder, the apocalypse, chaos.

Adams's great-grandfather, John Adams, could believe in a contest of powers, in a government where absolute authority was given to none but where the faculties of conscience and judgment belonged to all. In Henry Adams's view, this democratic ideology had its base in the natural conflict between rival forces, a conflict that pointed only to destruction, dissolution, or the triumph of the strongest force—a very dark prospect, yet it represents the dilemma of naturalist thinking in a democratic culture. Since Adams's social sensibility remained alive, it turned away from freedom to an idealization of unity in which power and value were miraculously at one with each other. He could imagine such a totalitarian fusion in the thirteenth-century power of the Virgin, maternal and sexual, the legitimacy of whose force *and* right were manifest. Or else he could kneel to the Dynamo of the twentieth century, whose power looked raw and savage because of its merely technological apparatus of control. Without the Virgin and her secret of sex, it was impossible for a naturalist to know where values come from. Therefore he faced the Virgin and the Dynamo and said in effect: one of you must rule us. His preference was obvious, and in making his choice he symbolizes, for several intellectual generations, a legacy of choices among the cults of vitalist power that have deeply affected the art and literature, the revisionist religions, and the naturalist politics of the twentieth century.

4 The Dehumanization of Politics

A Struggle Not of Men But of Forces

The Education and *Mont-Saint-Michel and Chartres* are imaginative achievements because of Henry Adams's capacity to project his personal sensibility into history, public affairs, art, philosophy, religion, and science. His interests are catholic, and we read him, much as his "nieces" must have listened to him, as if the voice speaking were that of human history itself. This is possible because his was a curiously detached personality, one that never forces his deeper private mind or private experience on the reader. Through choice, or through events, or through a combination of character and circumstances, his own role in public affairs became that of spectator, student, after-hours advisor, or teatime consultant. This detachment gave him license to color his reports of events with his own esthetic and ethical reflections, but, strangely, he denied that capacity of response to the agents in the drama. We can say that Adams liked to define persons in a categorically abstract sense but dismissed the ability of historical personages, such as Gladstone and Grant, to explain themselves and their motives.

That he did so was perhaps dictated by his major assumption that "Modern politics is, at bottom, a struggle not of a man but of forces" (*E*421). It may be that the tendency to view one's enemy, whether in war or in politics, as an abstraction is universal. The question is, what happens when political thought *begins* with the abstractions typical of a naturalist theory of "forces," particularly when, as in modern politics, these abstract forces bear the names of nation, race, and class? The paradoxical effect of the depersonalization of politics may be to increase the burden of prejudice that these abstract forces have to carry. Certainly, Adams gives evidence of this in his obsessive hatred of usurious finance, symbolized most often by the "gold-bug Jew." Is it easier to hate forces rather than men? This is difficult to say, but the premise that "forces" need to be ruled or resisted or overcome effectively eliminates the need for interpersonal recognitions and, as a consequence, the moral responsibility governing them. Or else these functions may become those of hindsight. In naturalist politics, defined as the struggle of forces, not of men, and presumably to be studied as a science, all the important judgments appear to be those made by observers and students. The serious consequence is that the actual participants are made to seem to act apart from judgment or to be ruled by rigid prejudgment or prejudice. "Forces" do not judge; they act and create judgment. Therefore, *during* a political event, which usually takes the form of conflict and can be violent, the agents are not only assumed to be pawns of the "forces" involved in the struggle; they are also encouraged to give themselves up to those forces, leaving it to history to express the legitimacy or right of that struggle.

This view of agents as instrumental and passive, while force remains the motor of events, is a marked characteristic of Adams's general thought, whether he was reflecting on politics, history, or education. In stating the goal of education he says this: "The young man himself, the subject of education, is a certain form of energy; the object to be gained is economy of his force" (*E* xxx). One doubts that young men were intended to recognize themselves in this description; as always, Adams's intention was to shock, and that, as well as his ironic, ruminative sensibility, is what makes his work so readable. Nevertheless, he was serious in that premise, at least as serious as he was in dealing with the Virgin, herself a divine expression of energy.

One is tempted to stress the contrast with earlier New England writers, for, in describing man as a form of energy and life as an economy of force, Adams might have been verifying the prophetic insight of Thoreau, who dramatized a similar reduction in the aphorism "Men have become the tools of their tools." Perhaps Adams was as ironic as Thoreau; but he accepted his vision, whereas Thoreau did not. It is all the easier, then, to see that reductive abstraction, in this typical American use, is the opposite face of transcendentalism, with its claim to a *magnified* image of life and humanity.

It is again as if he remembered a vivid image used by Thoreau when Adams described himself, the subject of an education, as a manikin which must be clothed: "The manikin, therefore, has the same value as any other geometrical figure of three or more dimensions, which is used for the study of relations . . .; it is the only measure of motion, of proportion, of human condition" (*E* xxx).[1] Thoreau called this manikin what it was, a lifeless puppet, a scarecrow: "Passing a cornfield the other day, close by a hat and coat on a stake, I recognized the owner of the farm."[2] And of course Thoreau felt that the right education would flesh such a scarecrow or that the scarecrow represented a man who had sacrificed his essential humanity to the conventional and utilitarian forms represented by the garments. But Adams was forced to conclude that in "education" clothes were everything.

The contrast is worth pursuing briefly to Emerson, who began all his discourse by saying, "The man must be so much that he must make all circumstances indifferent" (*ECW* 2:61). Adams neatly reverses this assertion, and his answer to Emerson is specific: "the forces of nature capture man" (*E* 474). To be captured by nature is an experience Emerson could understand and welcome, but not in the sense that Adams meant. The combination of surrender and self-assertion was one of the happy miracles of the Romantic view of nature, but it prepared the way for less benign views. Emerson particularly expressed a most congenial form of passive determinism: "We lie in the lap of immense intelligence, which makes us receivers of its truth and organs of its activity" (*ECW* 2:64). It was inspiration, or intelligence, that emanated from nature's stream of force in Emerson's view; and with nature's energy thus taking form in the individual mind and will, Emerson could say that character is the central reality: "Character, reality, reminds you of nothing else; it takes place of the whole creation" (*ECW* 2:61).

This anthropocentric spirit, which put up a barrier against either megalomania or solipsism, is the essence of Emerson and is the quality that made him so attractive to his own generation. Adams grew up on familiar terms with great men and was not in awe of them; but he was in awe of power. Power, not intelligence or inspiration, was what powerful men took from nature. The leaders who were successful were "forces of nature, energies of the prime, like the Pteraspis" (*E* 265). The fact that they existed, he said, made short work of scholars like himself: "The fact was certain; it crushed argument and intellect at once." To those who had succeeded in politics (in obvious contrast with himself) "action was the highest stimulant," and their "energies were the greater, the less they wasted on thought."

To judge the men of power reductively was perhaps inevitable in naturalist thought, but in Adams it vies with its opposite, a latent awe or hero worship that anticipates a supreme leader. Adams's actual example of the imperial power to rule was the Virgin, presented with high royal coloring in *Mont-Saint-Michel*. The Virgin was supreme because she could arouse a faith as strong as her own natural force. But could there not be other powers, semidivine, but capable of ruling with an authority derived from the "struggle of forces" in nature and history? Like his brother Brooks, Adams turned to the themes of race, nationality, and economics. In 1898 he wrote to Brooks while he was traveling in Hungary and looking across the border at autocratic Russia, which fascinated him with a vision of the future. He had been taught by his brother that "All monopolies will be assumed by the State, as a corollary to the proposition that the common interest is supreme over the individual."[3] Here was historic inevitability supplanting commercial democracy—which had once been another "inevitability"—and making itself "right" in the process. Adams's conclusion is summary.

> Not that I love Socialism any better than I do Capitalism, or any other Ism, but I know only one law of political or historical morality, and that is that the form of Society which survives is always in the Right; and therefore a statesman is obliged to follow it, unless he leads. Progress is Economy!

The future declares itself "right," but Adams still kept the privilege of withdrawal, a highly characteristic response; the socialism of the future was something with which he "seriously wishes [he] may have nothing to do." To this extent the fastidious determinist could withdraw from history, as indeed he seemed to, embracing failure as his excuse. And yet Adams could not rest with the conclusion that, on the terms of naturalist and historic fatalism, beliefs are only superimposed on the historic process. The greatest confidence of belief seemed to accompany victory in historic conflict. The sequence was perhaps as mysterious as the coincidence of Calvinist divine election with the signs of that election in the prosperity and conventional virtue of the believer. With his usual quickness Adams saw such Puritans in contemporary Marxists. As he wrote to Brooks, he was ready to accept the Marxist law of economy as the law of history, along with Brooks's own theory, laid on the same foundation. But then he added,

> They are a droll set of *plus que petits bourgeois*, these socialists, but they have all the truth there is; that is, belief in themselves.[4]

In part this was mere cynicism, but Adams did admire imperial belief systems, like the Virgin's rule or Constantine's quick-witted grasp of the utility of the Christian faith. His own faith that an energy in history commanded these developments illustrates a dualism installed at the center of naturalist thought. One half of this dualism is deeply passive, submitting thought and choice to the dominant movement of history. The other, in contrast, assumes a kind of automatic conformity with the will of history and so becomes completely willful itself, in the manner of the leader who believes that he can and must control men's minds in order to empower them with the beliefs that change history. The result is a kind of convenient dialogue between passive followers and the activist cadres who speak for history. The conflict between naturalist politics and the older democratic tradition makes itself most evident here.

In any case, and in a wider direction, beyond politics, naturalist fatality is a strong teacher, able to instruct both passivity and violence, both fanatic enthusiasm and stoic submission. The pattern characterizes a typical division in naturalist fiction between the emotions and intelligence, between actors and spectators, between aggressors and victims. The ultimate intelligence should be purely rational in the service of science or of neoscientific convictions. But the data of experience are ultimate also, in their violence or in some other emphatic demonstration of being. This violence is rich enough in its implications for politics, following from its wider meaning for naturalist literature and culture. Intensities of violence are linked in a frame of abstract causality. No excess is unreasonable as long as it is subject to the controlling hand of history—or to the novelist. The latter, as artist, can assume the moral immunity of history, with imagination substituting for fate and with fictional form paralleling historical truth. There are curious analogies in modern political history: esthetic values cross with politics, and both replace ethics; that is, the springs of action are energy and the genius for order.

Adams's Democracy

In his didactic political novel, *Democracy*,[5] Adams led his protagonist, Mrs. Lee, on his own road of discovery. She begins with the problem of moral evaluations. She goes to Washington, she says, because "I must know whether America is right or wrong" (*D* 49). But what she equally wanted was to watch the conflict of interests in the democracy and even to gain some share for herself in the control of "power":

> What she wished to see, she thought, was the clash of interests, the interests of forty millions of people and a whole continent, centering at Washington; guided, restrained, controlled, or unrestrained and uncontrollable, by men of ordinary mould; the tremendous forces of government, and the machinery of society, at work. What she wanted was *POWER*. [*D* 18]

And so she invites the corrupt Senator Ratcliffe, one of the masters of Washington, to pay court to her. She seems as morally obtuse as Gladstone in going a good deal of the way with Ratcliffe, accepting his political manipulations and even contemplating marriage for the sake of "*POWER*." Indeed, she becomes a rather unpleasant character in the cold self-righteousness with which she denounces Ratcliffe at the end; here Adams seems to have failed to

achieve novelistic detachment. He is himself Mrs. Lee judging politics; and it is instructive that she who has been in awe of power suffers for it when she fails to bring her equally strong need for being
"right" into relation with it.

The contradiction in Mrs. Lee's mind and behavior expresses the
ethical dilemmas of naturalist thought. The naturalist on the one
hand desires to accept the world on its own terms, including the
assumption that society is like a machine, one that is operated by
"tremendous forces" that are probably uncontrollable, at least by
men of "ordinary mould." But running counter to this, and producing an acute ambivalence, there remains within the naturalist
an undiminished urge to judge, to decide whether this or that man,
event, or institution is "right or wrong." Thus the reductive
simplicity of thinking in terms of "forces" invites a more sweeping,
and certainly a more unforgiving, moral judgment than one that
might be applied to true—and hence complex—moral agents.
Senator Ratcliffe, in his moral character, cannot be distinguished
from the type of man he represents or from the money interest or
the power interest he serves.

An illustration of Mrs. Lee's tendency to combine ethical and
naturalist judgments comes in this remark: "I really want to
know whether to believe in Mr. Ratcliffe. If I throw him over-
board, everything must go, for he is only a specimen" (D 50). One
man, though a senator, is to be judged as the representative of a
species. Apparently one doesn't question Ratcliffe as a person; one
questions the type, the institution, the society he represents, and
ultimately one questions nature itself or life. Mrs. Lee wants to
prove from things as they are in their natural existence, from
events in their historical process, whether man is a moral or a base
creature. The ethical questioning is superimposed on a naturalist
and determinist fatalism and directed at an abstract entity. Accordingly, the novel suffers a damaging loss of credibility, in both
human and literary terms, when Mrs. Lee turns on Ratcliffe, the
man she has been prepared to marry, with a generalized indignation that seems to be addressed to ideological abstractions and their
"specimens."

The problem was democracy before it was Senator Ratcliffe, and,
as she put it to herself, "What aspiration could she help to put into
the mind of this great million-armed monster that would make it
worth her love and respect?" (D 14). But almost on the same page
she is made to phrase the problem in the language of political
physics:

> She wanted to see with her own eyes the action of primary forces;
> to touch with her own hand the massive machinery of society; to

measure with her own mind the capacity of the motive power.
[*D* 17]

Ethics and science are going hand in hand, and Mrs. Lee is hardly
the protagonist to make a satisfactory resolution of their opposite
interests. The result is a highly typical confusion, one deeply
characteristic of modern politics, in which social abstractions, presented with the aura of scientific truth, begin to play a role in an
elaborate moral allegory. What Mrs. Lee wanted from Senator Ratcliffe, and the reductive role she finally forced him to play in her
imagination, can be illustrated from her early monologue with herself, before she entered the Washington world:

> Religion? . . . she could see no chance for a new faith of which she
> was to be the inspired prophet. Ambition? High popular ideals?
> Passion for whatever is lofty and pure? The very words irritated
> her. Was she not herself devoured by ambition, and was she not
> now eating her heart out because she could find no one object
> worth a sacrifice? [*D* 14]

For someone like Mrs. Lee to find nothing or no one worth a
sacrifice implies that nothing is worthy of consideration or respect.
Religious emotions are absolute, as we see in Adams himself, whose
imagination only the Virgin of Chartres could satisfy. But such an
imagination was stretched to its extremes by the conflict between
his traditional ethical values and his own respect for power,
coupled with his awe before science. Mrs. Lee suggests the frustration of religious passions in her constant search for revelations
from nature and from the conflict of historic forces. Before she
went to Washington, her earliest conclusion about the powerful
people of New York—the producers of petroleum, oil, silver, and
gold—was that "They found nothing to hold them up" (*D* 15). And
so her actual search at the center of political power was for both
power and inspiration, presumably embodied in the same persons.
What held people up, she admits in advance, must be found in the
"action of primary forces," a motive power that must work, turning
the machinery. She had to measure it, she says, though she admitted that it was a great mystery.

But mystery is the beginning of faith. Mrs. Lee had no doubt expected to be disappointed by Senator Ratcliffe; he was the occasion
for proof, vulgar as he was from the start and cheap for being
found out in corruption. But that does not imply that she had
nowhere else to turn or that a more imposing figure, one whose
power was less petty in its means, could not win her devotion. The
pathos of democratic politics is that it indeed regularly offered such
compromised agents of power as Senator Ratcliffe. The dream in

Mrs. Lee's mind has, in effect, an antidemocratic thrust. It is a vision of leadership, a discipline of greatness that would never let itself be vulnerable to the charge of pettiness or corruption. Right must keep pace with power, power with right, or else one was left with no basis for faith. On the other hand, that nagging moral vulnerability illustrated by Senator Ratcliffe might be canceled by a sufficiently awesome "primary force." In brief, this was the flammable mixture—a conflict between ethical sentiment and naturalist realism—that made Mrs. Lee the significant harbinger of the modern political temperament. Abstract in her own mind, treated as an abstraction by her author, she nevertheless prefigures the combination of cynicism and moral prejudice with which Adams came to express his deep revulsions toward politics and his obsessions with race and nationality.

Race and Abstract Prejudice

A post-Darwinian historian, attempting in the nineteenth century to deduce the laws of history from science and studying every day the power rivalries of great nations, was inevitably attracted by cosmic ideas of race. Adams was certainly a kind of racist, as he was an imperialist, even if, in his ironically speculative writing (his letters reveal more intense feeling), these labels lose much of their political venom.

When it came to dealing with such a force as Russia, operating in late nineteenth-century power rivalries, Adams, conceding like everyone else the backwardness of the Russian people and the incompetence of their leaders, resorted to a scientific term, inertia, and to another newly popular scientific word, race, to explain the immensity of the Russian threat. "Inertia" referred to an object resisting movement by its mass, or it referred to a mass in motion resisting stoppage by its momentum. Reviewing the role of Russia in world politics, Adams saw chiefly its mass, and it filled him with dread. "Could inertia of race, on such a scale, be broken up, or take new form?" (*E* 409). Race was biological mass and weight, and it was this aspect of Russia that struck him as pure latency, "a sink of energy" beyond anything known in ancient or modern history. As mass, Russia fascinated him, for he thought he could use his measure of that force to prophesy the future. Europe, he said, had always greatly feared the Bear; but he himself was ready to compound that fear with a myth derived from naturalist imagery. So massive a gathering of latent force could not help but arouse a metaphysical awe:

The image was that of the retreating ice-cap—a wall of archaic glacier, as fixed, as ancient, as eternal, as the wall of archaic ice that blocked the ocean a few hundred miles to the northward, and more likely to advance. [*E* 411]

On that level, at the margin of the known physical universe, he gave himself up to the myth of race, adding his contribution to that branch of modern esoteric politics. While traveling and surveying the struggling energies of Hungarians and Poles on one side of the border and Russians on the other, he said:

Race ruled the conditions; conditions hardly affected race; and yet no one could tell the patient tourist what race was, or how it should be known . . .; yet, without the clue, history was a nursery tale. [*E* 411–12]

All readers have been impressed by Adams's sharp hits in historical prophecy, nowhere sharper than in his respect for Russia's latent power and his anticipation of its ultimate rivalry with America. It is also clear that, if the prognosis had to favor one side or the other, he was not made very confident "by the hasty and unsure acceleration of America." Perhaps in America there was too much will, too much conscious striving, whereas Russia moved with the silent inevitability of fate. He seemed to be implying that when he said, "the fatalism of Russian inertia meant the failure of American intensity" (*E* 439). Perhaps he thought that America, because it was a "technological invention," provided nothing like the biological force and unity he found in race. Race gave Russia not only its future but its past, which America implicitly did not have; for why else would a son of the Puritans and the American Revolution be forced to seek his ancestors in Normandy?

To find them there, Adams made his imaginative journey to the Middle Ages in *Mont-Saint-Michel and Chartres:*

A great age it was, and a great people our Norman ancestors . . . . Since then our ancestors have steadily declined and run out until we have reached pretty near the bottom . . . . They have lost their religion, their art and their military tastes. They cannot now comprehend the meaning of what they did at Mont-Saint-Michel . . . . So we get Boston.[6]

It is evident in *Mont-Saint-Michel* that Adams associated the Norman climax of art and religion with a warrior energy. The dramatized events are the conquest of England and Sicily and the great Crusades, and the dominant figures are William the Conqueror and Richard the Lion-Hearted. These framed his interest in the art and religion of the twelfth and thirteenth centuries, and he does not conceal how much the cults of Mary and courtly love were warrior cults. Conquering England and building Coutances and Mont-Saint-Michel were not contradictory but were effects of the same activating genius; and though Adams felt richly appreciative as he stood before those monuments, he thought of them as radiations of energy, components of force.

The essence of the matter is that Adams saw the Normans as an imperial race. In doing so he liked to think that imperial power was a victory of unity over multiplicity, a fusion of the ideal and the actual, of art and experience, of reality and the imagination. The Norman warriors were too rough for Chartres, although the Virgin's medieval empire grew from their strength. Everything came together in the cathedrals, an ideal marriage of masculine and feminine; and from the unity of the architecture to the unity of the civilization it was a direct step:

> From the roof of the Cathedral of Coutances over yonder, one may look away over the hills and woods, the farms and fields of Normandy, and so familiar, so homelike are they, one can almost take oath that in this, or the other, or in all, one knew life once and has never so fully known it since. [*MMC* 3]

The writing brings out clearly what many of Adams's generation felt in their fascination with empire and race. These were holistic terms that signified the full and integrated life, a perfect organization of value, instinct, and power. It was as much pastoral as imperial, one might say; for the vision was of life's harmony, blessed by the actualities of race and power.

But the context for this dream is important, as the best students of Adams's work, Ernest Samuels and Robert Mane, both point out.[7] Adams became a Norman, in aspiration at least, by way of reacting to the racial incoherence and moral disorder of modern Europe and America. Before rediscovering Normandy, he had been visiting London, and in his letters he fulminated against Lombard Street, the capital of "gold-bug civilization," and noted all about him the signs of cultural degeneracy (this, by now had become his almost reflexive response to New York, London, and Paris). To find Normandy was to verify these reactions. As Mane describes it,

> Coutances was different; it was Norman; it was English; it was un-Jewish. For one must realize, even if it comes as a shock, that the mainsprings of Adams's rather complex emotions at Coutances were racist, not artistic. [P. 86]

However, this racism claimed intellectual credentials. Race was one word for a concentration of human energy; civilization was another—one that described the fruitful exercise of an integrated energy. Art was simply a major expression of that energy, an expression parallel with military conquest, as his brother Brooks maintained in his *The Law of Civilization and Decay,* a book in whose genesis Henry had an unmeasured but definite share.[8] To appreciate the Normans as a conquering race was to deprecate the Jew, and Adams seems to have contracted anti-Semitism in its virulent form concurrently with his move into ancestor worship. The Jew was the supreme antithesis, a representation, his brother Brooks might say, of economic energy, or the surplus energy that a society "stored in the shape of wealth"; as usurer, the Jew could be seen as the enemy and rival of "the emotional, the martial, and the artistic types of manhood."[9] The power of money, though it was a real power in its effects, was empty of the actual values of civilization; it was, like the Jew, rootless and unattached to anything but itself—a power over power.[10] Writing from Paris during these years of the Dreyfus Affair, Adams observed that "the people one sees here are mere *désoeuvrés.* Except the Jews, they have nothing to hang on, not even lamp-posts nowadays."[11] Even some aspects of late Gothic architecture are illustrated by the Jew, and he called Renaissance baroque a Jewish "gold-bug" style, by which he meant it was a vulgar style, meant to satisfy sensual appetites.

This prejudice is not to be dismissed as totally irrational and arbitrary. The Jew represented the inhuman abstractness of Adams's own basic concept of power. The Jew could be everything one feared or disliked because power was in everything that needed control but continually resisted it. It was consistent that the power of the Jew in Adams's mind was quite simply the power of the international bankers. This power was absolute; for instance, they owned Chamberlain and Balfour and all the power in England.[12] "We are in the hands of the Jews. They can do what they please with our values."[13] That sentence leads directly to the point. The Jew was a power; he manipulated values, and he was divorced from, or was implicitly hostile to, all the values a man like Adams could recognize. Like most literary naturalists, Adams was the naturalist in shock, expressing a dramatic consciousness of the lost metaphysical harmony of the world and the breach between power and value. He himself called his inclinations those of a priest or monk, and he converted his scientific understanding to priestly use. Did he worship power? Or, given his temperament, did he not rather hate and fear it as something barren and violent? We know that he used it to construct a demonology as well as a divinity of power symbols. Everywhere he looked in his day, power was in the wrong hands, used for exploitation and profit, damned by a vulgar greed, and presiding over the contemporary decadence of art, religion, and aristocratic virtues like those of the Norman knight.

So it was that the Jew emerged in Adams's imagination at the same time that he discovered the cult of the Virgin Mary. If she was the source and symbol of value-breeding inspirations, the Jew was the traditional symbol of her antithesis. In Adams's case one apparently did not have to believe in Christ in order to believe in the Virgin. Similarly, one did not need Christ to believe in the anti-Christ.

Adams's form of anti-Semitism is prophetic of the way race theory attaches itself to the metaphysics of power and to ambiguous alternations between moral and amoral judgment. History is driven by "forces," as yet not entirely understood and perhaps never to be understood; but the temptation remains to dramatize a struggle and personify an evil. Conflict is everywhere, but the enemy has a blank face. Power, in this mode of thought, becomes deeply devious and conspiratorial, and those who wield power become less-than-human embodiments of "forces." It is easier, however, to see the agents of power as human enough to be hated or feared or fought but not human enough to be dealt with on the level of moral communication. Naturalist politics reflects the psychology of war, or universalizes it. The fight for survival is a naturalist conflict in which either the enemy has no traits except as a power that must be resisted or, if he has human traits, they are colored and distorted by mystification. The determinist fatalism of naturalist politics draws the portrait of an agent whose motives are certain in only one respect: that they can never be reconciled with one's own interests. In other words, the enemy is incorrigible and fatal; either he will destroy us or we must destroy him.

Making power abstract and identifying with it the human agents who wield it or are the objects of it leads inevitably to making humanity abstract. When, therefore, the power conflict becomes so intense that moral judgments of it can no longer be made, it is almost certain that the shadow of paranoia will fall over it. To talk about forces rather than men is to liberate rather than restrain the imagination of conspiracies. This may be a general tendency, as if the depersonalization of history creates the need for interior personifications that attach themselves to abstractions of race, class, and nation. The depersonalization of moral judgments does not lead to their disappearance but to their magnification as political judgments. Instead of inferences from concrete events and actual persons, judgments are based on a priori considerations almost wholly preoccupied with an abstract entity called a "force" and an equally abstract process of necessary and universal "struggle."

Empire and Apocalypse

Nothing reveals the moral ambiguity of this pattern of political thought better than Adams's close emotional involvement with the Dreyfus case. France was, at the time, Adams's alternate home, where he spent part of every year, and what he saw in the Dreyfusard campaign was a conspiracy directed against the entire social and national structure of France. Not only the army but the people of France and the future of France would be condemned if Dreyfus were acquitted.

Therefore, although he was able to admit that Dreyfus was probably innocent, particularly at the time of his second trial and conviction, Adams felt that the justice or injustice of the matter had no weight when France could be ruined as a corporate national entity.[14] His choice for political survival rather than justice is instructive, for it suggests how far committed he himself was to the pragmatic use of power. Whether he employs the language of panic or cynicism, Adams admits in his letters of this time that his ancestors (from Yankee Americans back to Normans) had flourished through force: the force of the original Norman Conquest, that of treason (the American Revolution), and that of the suppression of treason (the Civil War). Power had given him his world, and power would defend it. In any case, he knew of worse immoralities than the Dreyfus injustice, and he cited to his correspondent the Boer War, which he called the "British Dreyfus." The remarkable thing is that he saw British imperialism as a "Jew interest," a part of the "great capitalist machine," which now included the Adams interest.[15]

Power at this level of conception is demonic; it requires the subordination of justice, and, whatever the interest on each side, "we must kill them [the Boers]," as he says in a letter, or be ruined.[16] This was his effort to dismiss moral cant, to accept a reality as hard as the granite coast of Normandy. But the confusion between "we" and "they," exaggerated by cynicism in these passages from his letters, sometimes seems complete; for, on the one hand, his world must be defended against the Jews, but, in the same group of letters, *his* world is admitted to be that of anti-Boer England and of America—both now, according to him, controlled by the Jews. Could it be that the power that accused and imprisoned Dreyfus was *also* Jewish?

Such absurdities lead to the main point, which seems to be that power has become the object of superstitious fear, incapacitating judgment. Whose power is in me—a power that I defend—and whose power is it that I oppose? Adams found his interests and those of his family defended by a system that he hated; he found the same force present in opposed interests; and everywhere he found the same negative principle of force, which finally exacerbated him to the point where he shared the impulse to violence with a street mob searching for a Rothschild and a lamppost. So he expressed himself in letters from Paris at the height of the Dreyfus conflict.[17]

To that source of demoralization we must add a more abstract panic, one that Adams felt as he observed national and imperial conflict everywhere and prepared himself for the apocalypse that his view of history demanded. Writing to Mrs. Cameron at the time of the second Dreyfus trial, when there was a strong possibility that Dreyfus would be acquitted and set free, Adams sounds almost plaintive:

> Dreyfus is to be set free...but what is to become of France? They can't acquit Dreyfus without condemning France, and what happens after a moral *débâcle* worse than Sedan?... France must subside into a dependency on central Europe. Then what is to become of us?...how are we to deal with a united Europe bent on mastering Asia which means the world? Our people are not even at a point to begin asking questions. They can't even manage the Philippines. They don't want to think about it.[18]

This letter is a classic expression of what might be called Great War psychology: "a *débâcle*," "what is to become of us," "France must subside," "mastering Asia, which means the world." Such phrases remind us of other voices heralding war and crisis in this century. The defeat of France by the Jews in the Dreyfus Affair would mean that France would become socialist or else an appendage of central Europe. In the same letter, Adams elaborated his sense of power fatalities by agreeing with Admiral Dewey that "we" must "by the nature of things be at war" with central Europe. "We" were America and England, and behind both "us" and "them" there was a ubiquitous force that took both sides or, rather, used them. With hindsight we can see that this was the view taken by many before and during World War I, a view of shifting rivalries and threats that led to slaughter, which Adams in these passages seems to predict.

Perhaps the war was only the self-fulfilling prophecy of such minds. If peoples, nations, and races were all caught in the natural rivalry of power and survival, and if this principle was ultimate, all other values being shunted aside, the result might very well be a blind conflict in the dark. The face of the enemy changes, the battle shifts and reverses sides. For instance, in another stream of prophecy Adams saw England—the old enemy of his family and of the youthful United States—falling into the American system. Then France joined what he now called the Atlantic system, defensively, as a guard against Germany and the Central Powers. But then, swept up by the momentum of his theory, he speculated about the new threat from Russia, the most mysterious and fearful of all. *That* threat might draw Germany into the Atlantic system, he says. The formula follows from the law of force, or the concentration of force in nations. The ultimate result might be that Russia could come into the combination, presumably against another threat. Apparently he meant Asia, and this great defensive combination of old enemies within the white race would be "the last and highest triumph of history" (*E* 439).

In this way the naturalist historian looked for an apotheosis in history, an ambiguous resolution (would it be salvation?) of an endless series of rivalries and recombinations. Force and war must be moralized somehow, perhaps as in a physical or chemical process that reaches equilibrium. The resemblance to Marxist ideology is fascinating, with the conflict of nations comparable to class conflict and the ultimate unity of the white race, "the last and highest triumph of history," rivaling the victory of the proletariat and its triumph in classlessness.

But Adams preferred the vision of apocalypse to utopia. The "triumphs of history" could be only transient. At best he could visualize another Roman empire. Or was it—horrors—going to be a Jewish empire? The latter possibility was a nightmare, the reverse of his dream, because power always shows the two faces of the sides in conflict. The race enemy, the national enemy, could become the reductive symbol of one's own reductive habit of mind. But such thoughts were reserved for Adams's private letters and his private mind. In his public writings he taught himself to contemplate historic conflict and even the threatened apocalypse with some equanimity and with more than stoic acceptance. If ultimate violence was ordained by natural and historic law, there might be some sentiment to dread it and to mourn its necessity but none to oppose it. Adams himself kept the prerogatives of a spectator of history; his vein of universalist speculation is always daring and always, or so it seemed, disinterested. Still, he wrote during the great age of American imperial expansion, when his intimate friend, John Hay, was secretary of state. Who knows precisely how much these theories of inevitable conflict, images of the fall of nations, and images of the apocalyptic "last triumph of history" haunted Cabinet rooms everywhere in the crucial years before

World War I? It is doubtful that we can separate cause and effect in the relationships between the political imagination and political reality. One thing is certain: fatalism can support faith as well as resignation, and faith and resignation both remain very important and calculable elements of force in every strategic equation of modern history. An era of history has not only been recorded by naturalist fatalists who resemble Adams; it has been enacted by equally fatalist politicians and ideologists. This we know from the violent record of the sixty-odd years since Adams's death.

The proof that determinism breeds its own form of inspiration exists in Adams's record of his life. When he came close to great affairs again, as close as the distance between his house on Lafayette Square and the home of John Hay next door, he could feel a deep exhilaration. The summer of the Spanish-American War he said, was the beginning of the Indian summer of his life. "He had reason to be more than content with it. Since 1864 he had felt no such sense of power and momentum, and had seen no such number of personal friends wielding it" (*E* 362). He was enjoying himself as he had in his youth, in London during the Civil War, when, as secretary to his father, the ambassador, he had felt an ecstasy of power.

He found history now fulfilling the oldest dream of the Adams family, "the object of bringing England into an American system." The chance was, he said, that Germany had suddenly appeared as the terror of Europe and had "frightened England into America's arms." But chance wasn't all—not for Adams; he had to sum up matters and give history a direction: "For the first time in his life, he felt a sense of possible purpose working itself out in history" (*E* 363). After watching so often the signs of disintegration in his own civilization, what he saw now was the chance to control power in its forward thrust, and he called it what it was: "empire-building":

> he could see that the family work of a hundred and fifty years fell at once into the grand perspective of true empire-building, which Hay's work set off with artistic skill. [*E* 363]

Empire was the word for historic success, for racial and national success; it was the visible sign of the concentration and mastery of energies. Adams's mind, detached as it was, gives us an outline of this imperialist logic as well as its accompanying apocalyptic emotions. His first principle was an abstract view of power itself, as if power worked outside human agencies, outrunning human responsibilities. When the Roman Empire fell, it was not through evil or weakness or error. It was, he said, explainable only by the law of accelerated energy. It was a problem in mechanics, not politics. The dynamic law in this case described an excess, not a deficiency, of energy, or an excess of action and reaction, and this had "to account for the dissolution of the Roman Empire, which should, as a problem of mechanics, have been torn to pieces by acceleration" (*E* 478).

But these great forces that could run out of control still offered the greatest of prizes. Hay's strategic victory over Russia and Germany in the Boxer War saved China from Europe, but not for a noble or benevolent sentiment; the point was, Adams thought, to put America at the center of world power:

> For a moment, indeed, the world had been struck dumb at seeing Hay put Europe aside and set the Washington Government at the head of civilization so quietly that civilization submitted, by mere instinct of docility, to receive and obey his orders. [*E* 392]

This was a heady experience to share with his dear friend and neighbor, but the mood could change as suddenly as Rome's destiny after Diocletian. As he examined America's trials of strength in a future contest with Russia, he knew the dread of impotence—for Hay, for himself, and for his country:

> One's mind goes far, and dreams much over such a field of vision, but in the end it always loses itself in Asia. Russia is omnipotence. Without Russia, such a scheme might fail. I fear Russia much! Why can one never penetrate that polar mystery?[19]

The "scheme" refers to the Adams's ancestral commitment to American hegemony in North and South America. Ironically, he was writing this in a letter to his brother Brooks, welcoming the publication of *The Law of Civilization and Decay*. Welcoming it, he still feared harm to society in "the expression of its logical conclusions":

> I look on our society as a balloon, liable to momentary collapse, and I see nothing to be gained by sticking pins through the oil canvas. I do not care to monkey with a dynamo.[20]

This letter is witness to a mental process, as dark as the mystery of Russia, where images of power march like ghosts in *Macbeth*, alternately beckoning toward either enterprise and conquest or total catastrophe. The imperial struggle was, on the one hand, inevitable and, on the other, catastrophic in its consequences. The side that won (in China, in Europe, in South America, it really didn't matter where) would rule the world; the side that lost would, if not extinguished, be ruled. This was Adams's imperialist logic; it was fatalistic and violent, and behind it was the self-immolating will of a Puritan naturalist submitting to the process of historical election. For lack of any better proof, one's virtue might be confirmed by victory. In any case, nothing much would survive defeat.

Whether he looked to imperial victory or defeat, Adams was an imaginative prophet in an age of apocalyptic thinking, dominated at one end by Marx and at the other by Spengler. Other than the Virgin of Chartres, to whom it was linked in the historicist formula, the apocalyptic theme most directly expresses his personal temperament. All readers of *The Education* and *Mont-Saint-Michel* must feel the persistence of this theme and the way it establishes the unique tone of these two works, which are marked by lively curiosity with an undertone of passive dread and melancholy, by cold pleasure in facing harsh truths, and by a stoic will to endure whatever comes, combined with a sometimes rueful, sometimes almost gleeful, acceptance of catastrophe.

In accepting catastrophe Adams often assumed the posture of a vindictive prophet, one who saw that the future would punish and who wished to emphasize that grim prospect for its purgative value. Apocalypse is in the voice of a Jeremiah who wants revenge against his own people for their sins, as in this letter Adams wrote in 1893, when financial collapse threatened him and his family:

> For my own part, hating vindictively, as I do, our whole fabric and conception of society, against which my little life has squeaked protest from its birth, and will yell protest till its death, I shall be glad to see the whole thing utterly destroyed and wiped away. With a communism I could exist tolerable well, for the commune is rather favorable to social consideration apart from wealth; but in a society of Jews and brokers, a world made up of maniacs wild for gold, I have no place.[21]

There is a certain amount of self-indulgence in these moods of violence, and when, in a facetious vein, Adams took to calling himself a "Conservative Christian Anarchist," it was a way of spelling out both his welcoming of the apocalypse and his reactionary feelings of nostalgia. He wished for destruction on behalf of Christian Conservative principles, but the main thing was to see the "goldbug" Jew order break down. Yet his hunger for apocalypse expressed more than a conservative's revenge, more than a playful herald's cry for the next cycle of history. Naturalist historicism insists on the omnipotence of the forces at work in history and, doing so, tends to insist, too, on the necessity of violence in the expected crises of change. The more determinist, the more apocalyptic, seems to be the rule; orthodox Marxists, for instance, never compromise the principle of the inevitability of revolution. The new society can grow only on the ruins of the old; otherwise one cannot be certain that the power agents in whom one believes, whether they are involved in the clash of races and nations or the conflict of classes, have been truly chosen by history. Violence is the sign that history will not wait, that its path is determined and inevitable.

The Virgin of Chartres represented, for Adams, the zenith of a curve of destruction and creation that measured Christianity's rule in history. And when Adams stood before the twentieth-century Dynamo, he felt an almost equal awe and the need of some new revelation. It might well be the product of a miracle or the announcement of a Second Coming:

> As Nature developed her hidden energies, they tended to become destructive .... The stupendous acceleration after 1800 ended in 1900 with the appearance of the new class of super-sensual forces, before which the man of science stood at first as bewildered and helpless as, in the fourth century, a priest of Isis before the Cross of Christ. [*E* 486–87]

Could this historic acceleration of destructive energies also be creative? The idea was interesting, and Adams might, with consistency, have become a revolutionary, though he chose the way of "conservative anarchism" instead. There was a note of suicide in this for a world that, as he said, "had lived too long." And if the world was only a machine, propelled by energy, then Adams seemed quite willing to see it run down; at least he got emotional satisfaction from saying yes to the majestic dictate of the law of entropy in physics.

But, above all, Adams asked for indictment and judgment from history, and Saint Michael himself could not come with fiercer judgment than the new forces of science:

> Power leaped from every atom, and enough of it to supply the stellar universe showed itself running to waste at every pore of matter. Man could no longer hold it off....

> An immense volume of force had detached itself from the unknown universe of energy, while still vaster reservoirs, supposed to be infinite, steadily revealed themselves. [*E* 494–95]

It may be that Adams was obsessed by the Second Law of Thermodynamics because it promised the inevitable extinction of such concentrations of energy. The evidence from these passages indicates that he was frightened by his own genie of power, summoned by his imagination. Yet fear is probably not the right word for the complex reactions of this man, who imagined the full impact of the twentieth century and the bursting of the atom. His writings are even more prophetic than that. What Adams reveals is a range of attitudes, moving from stoic identification with the thrust of history to a masochism inviting destruction, from an irresponsible exhilaration in the presence of violence to moods of cynical detachment, from postures of self-pity to a passive fatalism that finally pervaded all of his alternations of judgment and attitude. In the chameleon turns of his mind there is considerable intellectual pathos but at the same time a foreboding reflection of traits dominant in the political temperament of our century. Amateur scientist, amateur politician, Adams was primarily a man of letters, expressing a sensibility embedded in modern literary culture. As such, his work has become an indispensable prologue to a reexamination of that culture.

5 Naturalist Fiction and Political Allegory

Abstractions of Force—Tropisms of Need

No one discriminates a choice or a motive very clearly in Dreiser's *Sister Carrie*. The characters exhibit, rather, a kind of tropism of need in the midst of a stream of force. Because of this, the novel has a consistency that makes it a classic of American naturalist fiction, a tribute to Dreiser's single-mindedness in reducing human action to simple responses of attraction and repulsion. In the early chapters the theme of force attracting need stands out: Carrie and Drouet meet in the city, and the sex of one and the money of the other are the media of their exchange of power.

The city is itself an overwhelming quantification of power, "a roar of life" that dominates its human agents and objects. Actually, it is the city, with its promise of satisfied desire, that seduces Carrie, and Dreiser describes her responsive wish to "make it prey and subject—the proper penitent, grovelling at a woman's slipper."[1] It is characteristic that desire should be expressed in the language of conquest, yet this is no mere metaphor; for desire in *Sister Carrie* is conceived of as a force among forces that, as such, inevitably tend to pose the issue of surrender or conquest. But this abstraction of force, whether sexual or otherwise, is inseparable from real things, the things that Carrie sees and wants and that the city provides: lights, food, handsome clothes, fine houses. Things are in the foreground of her attention, not people and certainly not her own passions. Her seduction is preceded by a good dinner at a good restaurant, and Drouet's presence is epitomized in the flashing of his gold cuff-links. The scene is intended to support the author's declaration that "man is the victim of forces over which he has no control." Though Carrie is herself a force, certainly as Drouet and Hurstwood know her, and perhaps a central force in the city, she is still a victim:

> She could not realize that she was drifting, until he secured her address. Now she felt that she had yielded something—he, that he had gained a victory . . . . Already he took control. [*SC* 10]

But no one really has control, as we shall soon see, although the issue of victory and defeat remains alive. This is naturalism in its simplest expression: there is a contest; success and failure are real; but the conscious will, or conscience, is most obvious in its subordination. Carrie's conscience

> was no just and sapient counsellor . . . . It was only an average little conscience, a thing which represented the world, her past environment, habit, convention, in a confused way. With it, the voice of the people was truly the voice of God. [SC 82]

In some instances that voice might be strong, but there is always a stronger:

> She was alone; she was desireful; she was fearful of the whistling wind. The voice of want made answer for her. [SC 83]

Want is a strong power; it is located in the human person, but reduction makes it abstract. What *is* purely human may be "the voice of the people," here rendered as the voice of God, himself a habit and a convention. The interesting result is to assign human force to mental fictions and to move toward nonhuman terms for describing forces with greater potency and a greater claim on reality. The lights of the city have as strong an influence as the light in Drouet's eyes, Dreiser writes. But since we are directly told that Carrie felt only a minimal sexual attraction to Drouet, though "she felt that she liked him," it is plausible to judge that he is only the point of focus for the series of radiating "forces" that meet her in the city. On the very first pages Dreiser sets the terms for Carrie's "fall":

> Half the undoing of the unsophisticated and natural mind is accomplished by forces wholly superhuman. [SC 6]

In that sense, the sex drive impelling Drouet must be considered to be as "superhuman" as the power inherent in the crinkly ten-dollar bills he presses on Carrie at a strategic moment.

In this world, things that money can buy speak more eloquently than people, who hardly speak at all. Thus Drouet communicates to Carrie:

> As he cut the meat, his rings almost spoke. His new suit creaked. He was a splendid fellow. [SC 54]

And yet, with all the respect that goes to suits and rings, and for all the directness of their impact on Carrie, who is indeed attracted to them as by a magnet (the chapter title is "The Magnet Attracting: A Waif amid Forces"), the reader is simultaneously made aware that such things are symbols. Clothes are the signs of sexual value. They are indeed indispensable to it and to status as well, and Dreiser sums up Drouet by saying that good clothes are so essential to his composition that without them he is nothing. For the rest, he owned a strong physical nature—meaning a sexual drive—a love for various pleasures, and "the company of successful men."

Dreiser suggests that the other men in Carrie's life are more complex (the novel plots a curve from simplicity to complexity), but Hurstwood and Ames are hardly better able to transcend Dreiser's abstractions of force and desire. Ames represents Carrie's vague aspirations for something better; he comes from the sphere of education and culture, another frontier for Carrie to cross. Hurstwood, for all the simple power with which he is drawn and the overwhelming sense of social gravity in his fall, is the symbol of worldly poise and the prestige of the businessman's role and relationships. In fact, he is the symbol of nothing more than the idea of success, as he later becomes the symbol of worldly failure.

This rapid movement from the realism of facts, objects, and simple responses to symbolic abstraction is a significant characteristic of traditional naturalist fiction. There is no mystery in this; it is the direct consequence of a theoretical hunger that grows as fast as the mountain of detail heaped up by realist reporting. Things like Carrie's skirt or Drouet's rings are attractive in themselves as objects of desire or need, but they almost immediately become symbols of the power they generate, and *that* is their value.

This naturalist tradition obviously reflects the social symbol-making of a society of producers and consumers. Subordinating other values, things become the signs of the power asserted in gaining them. And so a simple desire or need is translated into a sign of the power needed to satisfy it. This tautological circle may be characteristic of a society given up to "conspicuous consumption," but here the chief point is to note the emphasis it receives in naturalist fiction and the way it is used to elaborate a structure of power values in that fiction.

Such values are allowed to overwhelm or even exclude distinguishing features of character. The discriminated qualities of Carrie as a person are subordinated to the sexual power she generates, first over Drouet, "the creature of an inborn desire" that urged him toward women "as a chief delight." Hurstwood is another helpless "moth of the lamp," who, unable to give up Carrie, sacrifices his established "success" for her. This is a bad tradeoff for him, since he loses what it was that gave him sexual power over Carrie in the first place. One might say that Hurstwood is the victim not so much of poor judgment as of his own insufficient power resources. It is clear that he cannot have Carrie without losing all his property to his wife and probably his job as well. The result is the abortive theft and flight, ending in the loss of his money, his job, his status, and, eventually, Carrie and his life. The drama could be called a specific example of naturalist tragedy, where, instead of an even exchange, one power cancels another, and a sexual force generated by Carrie engulfs and lays waste all the power that Hurstwood could claim as his own.

That power was money, and in simple seriousness Carrie understands that at the start. She holds what Drouet gave her in her hands, "two soft, green, handsome ten-dollar bills.... It was something that was power in itself" (*SC* 57). It was, indeed, "stored energy," a truth that reaches its dismal climax in the scenes describing Hurstwood's decline and fall, where Dreiser seems to count the gradual, almost dollar-by-dollar disappearance of Hurstwood's money. As Hurstwood declines to a physical shadow, losing all interest in Carrie, the accompanying refrain is the absence of money to buy meat or pay the rent. Although Carrie deserts his bed at that point, her action is not given any more emphasis, by either of them, than his failure to pay the rent.

However, once the issue is clearly power—and both sex and money become symbols of power conflict—the naturalist writer has access to dramatic significance and can escape the threat of triviality. The limitations on his resources for depicting character and action remain severe, but human experience can now be made meaningful by the use of at least one, and sometimes all, of three characteristic patterns: the pathos of victimization; abstraction of the characters as agents of a social or a biological force; and melodramatic violence. Violence is of course inevitable in fictional representations of power conflicts, but one of its advantages is the way it can link simplifications of motive to exaggerations of action, exaggerations that are quantitative, not qualitative, in their measure of power. Thus Hurstwood, almost stupid in the commonplace quality of his infatuation, commits a crime, breaking with all his previous life, in order to win Carrie. His eventual decline and suicide are the end products of the slow progression of that violence in his life, a violence buried beneath the problems of paying the rent and buying steak for dinner. Carrie herself is first a victim, then a survivor, and, finally, a winner, but Minna Hooven, in Norris's *The Octopus,* illustrates the latent melodrama in Carrie's sexual career. Minna has the choice of starving on the street or succumbing to prostitution. Her mother, separated from her on the streets of San Francisco, literally does starve to death. The diminished scale of characterization here is counterbalanced by accentuated pathos, by the vivid outline of social forces in action, and, above all, by the sharp impact of violence.

On the other hand, even the most extreme violence arouses a relatively minor response in naturalist characters. Emotions must not be complex or profound, though needs or wants may be drastic compulsions to act. Subjective experience is thus submerged by the imperatives of action, and neoscientific abstractions, whether of poverty or sex, dominate personal response. People are the creatures of natural and social forces. They must be kept from breaking though the thesis that controls them. It is stressed at the beginning that Carrie has a "rudimentary mind," and Norris's McTeague is almost an ape in his exaggerated animal sensibility; the instinctive and conditioned behavior of both is thus made more visible. The work of Dos Passos is characteristically naturalist, for, large and comprehensive as the world he describes may be, it is a world in which human sensibility is absent or is very early aborted.

It should be noted, however, that the emotional and intellectual retardation that characterizes the people of orthodox naturalist fiction serves an ideological point. The stunting of life becomes the ground for moral accusation: the poor can *afford* emotions no more than pleasure. We remember Minnie, Carrie's sister, and her husband Hanson in their dour puritan life of work, forbidding Carrie the chance to go to the theater. And Carrie herself really enjoys nothing so much as her moments as an actress, when she seems to come to life; it is as if both emotional and imaginative experience were restricted to fantasy, to life on the stage. The major effect of this on the reader is to make him sense a generalized repression, a universal poverty, in which all imaginative needs become one. Whether it is nature or society that has dictated this restraint, the weight is sensed as unbearable. One of the most relevant and expressive revolutionary slogans of our time was voiced in May 1968, when the French students wrote on their walls, "All power to the imagination."

To sum up, one can say that a study of literary naturalism leads to a series of paradoxes. A literature devoted ostensibly to the reporting of reality is found to be based on abstraction, allegory, and melodrama. The theme of power is in itself a simplistic abstraction of values. Dreiser accurately makes money its chief symbol. Money is undefined latent power; what you do with it is another matter. At the same time, money is the sign of success, the specialized status of power; and what money will buy provides further, secondary, signs: fine clothes, houses and carriages, the company of successful men and women, all of which, as Dreiser points out, both Hurstwood and Drouet need as much as they need sexual gratification or any other simple want.

More direct and tangible signs of power are communicated in the melodrama of the contest itself, no matter what is won or lost. Every desire or motive, and particularly sex, is faced by a contest, as when Carrie, at her first meeting with Drouet, feels that "she had yielded something, he had gained a victory." This may be petty realism, but the theme of life as a contest leads to greater exaggerations, as in *The Octopus,* in the brutal confrontations between the wheat ranchers and the railroad. Frank Norris was in fact the most melodramatic of naturalists, and he expressed his convictions as follows:

> Terrible things must happen . . . . They [the characters] must be twisted from the ordinary, wrenched out from the quiet, uneventful round of every-day life, and flung into the throes of a vast and terrible drama that works itself out in unleashed passions, in blood, and in sudden death.[2]

The statement is revealing, since one might suppose that the extraordinary and the grotesque do not embody the truth that naturalism seeks. It tells us, in part, that sensationalism compensates for the dullness of ordinary lives and of weak or incapacitated people. This is a literary need, and melodrama hovers over the pages of every naturalist novel; but this need is reinforced by naturalist thought. Exaggerated violence and victimization can prove a thesis of social conflict or demonstrate a historic truth that might be apocalyptic or redemptive. Marx himself was a "scientist" of the apocalypse, and his habit of combining realistic documentation with melodramatic finalities provides a close analogy with naturalist fiction.

Such marks of the apocalypse are clear traits of naturalist writing, as I shall observe later. The more subtle and paradoxical result of dealing obsessively with ordinary experience is the tendency to allegorize human types behind the mask of realism. Frank Norris again exhibits this trait more visibly than other naturalist writers. His pages are dominated by stereotypes, themselves melodramatic, of the poet, the banker, the western rancher, the man of the soil, the woman of the sexual soil, the miser of money, the miser of power. An example of the stereotype that becomes a caricature is Zerkow, the Jewish miser in Norris's *McTeague,* who achieves a degree of grotesqueness the author could not have intended:

> He was a dry, shrivelled old man of sixty odd. He had the thin, eager, cat-like lips of the covetous; eyes that had grown keen as

those of a lynx from long searching amidst muck and debris; and clawlike, prehensile fingers—the fingers of a man who accumulates, but never disburses. It was impossible to look at Zerkow and not know instantly that greed—inordinate, insatiable greed—was the dominant passion of the man.[3]

The obsessively animal metaphor here seems clearly prompted by the need to abstract a force, to locate it in nature, and, at the same time, to pronounce a moral judgment on it. The passage illustrates, in Norris's vein of caricature, an ideological compulsion to focus on the simplest, clearest forces in any zone of conflict.

Winners and Losers

Hurstwood attracts Carrie because he demonstrates all the signs of a successful man, "reflecting in his personality the ambitions of those who greeted him" (*SC* 150). Even his grace and suavity (which are his best qualities, Carrie notes) emanate from his success. The most impressive thing about him is his vocation as a professional master of ceremonies and greeter of the prosperous patrons of his elegant saloon. He "knew by name . . . hundreds of actors, merchants, politicians, and the general run of successful characters about town" (*SC* 41). And, when he falls, in the second half of the novel, it is, in the largest sense, because he has lost his vocation: the function of greeting success and sharing in it.

The strong effect of Dreiser's novel results from his dynamic sense of the curve of fortune, a simple graph of the rise and fall of power. Thus the structure of *Sister Carrie* is based on the closest possible contrast between Carrie's rise and Hurstwood's fall, and human relations are dictated by the accompanying view of life as a contest for success and a struggle for survival. To a large extent, as I have said, the judgment of success is tautological: success is what succeeds, as when Hurstwood's friends see in him only the reflection of their own ambitions. Dreiser was no doubt viewing the American city realistically when he saw that success there was its own excuse for being, no matter how achieved. But imaginatively, and for his own purposes, Dreiser adopted the success cult of American life by emphasizing its intrinsic force, as if the capacity to succeed were a quality inherent in some people and not in others. In Dreiser, success is not based on a gradual consensus among people. It is not a valuation at all but a force that seizes the judgment of others and compels their submission. When Carrie has her first success on the stage, for instance, the effect on her is described this way:

> She was now experiencing...that subtle change which re-
> moves one out of the ranks of the suppliants into the lines of the
> dispensers of charity. She was, all in all, exceedingly happy. [*SC*
> 165]

With "the independence of success...with the tables turned, she
was looking down, rather than up, to her lover" (*SC* 161).

This turning of the tables is a motif that unifies Dreiser's story.
The men in Carrie's life succeed each other in cycles: as one goes
up, the other goes down. Hurstwood supplants Drouet, Ames replaces Hurstwood, each on the basis of some vaguely cited
superiority in a competitive struggle. These comparisons of
strength apply also to Carrie herself, who eventually is destined to
look down from a pinnacle. The men, as they appear in the story,
are stronger than she is; she then grows as if by absorbing their
strength. This cycle is incomplete at the end, for Ames, the third
man in Carrie's life, is defined only by comparisons, such as, "He
seemed wiser than Hurstwood, saner and brighter than Drouet" (*SC*
271). (Comparisons had begun earlier, with simpler values, as when
Carrie notes her preference for Hurstwood's soft leather shoes
over Drouet's patent leather.) The reader never quite sees *what* is
strong or wise or sane in Ames and may conclude that all values are
comparative and stand for quantity, not substance, in the strangely
abstract world of this naturalist novel.

The success of an actress is of course plausibly based on her
ability to magnetize an audience, but it is suggestive that Dreiser
limits his description of Carrie's gift to its effect on others. Her
talent *is* the power she has over an audience, and it may consist more
of chemistry than of art. Dreiser makes an explicitly parallel point
about failure in his theory of "katastates," the chemical poisons
generated by failure, which create depression and mental and
physical deterioration (*SC* 274). Failure, like success, is a part of
animal fate, and the least superstitious view of it is to refer it to
biological old age, which Dreiser does to reinforce the more imaginative hypothesis of the chemistry of failure, which he had
borrowed from a contemporary experimenter in physiological
psychology.[4]

Thus Hurstwood's case illustrates the aging cycle: there is youthful flourishing and old decay, and the balance at middle age—
where we find Hurstwood at the beginning of the story—can only
tilt downward toward the grave. The cycle, and the sexual rivalry
that it includes, is mirrored in the relation between Hurstwood and
his wife; his taking of Carrie represents a biological defeat for her,
and her bitterness is largely a response to that: "She was fading

while he was still preening himself in his elegance and youth" (*SC* 177).

Her straightforward self-defense is to use her power over their money, and the chapter heading for Hurstwood's struggle with his wife, "Flesh Wars with Flesh," is not an exact description; for the mortified flesh of Mrs. Hurstwood takes comfort and revenge from the equally strong power of money, a kind of a variation on the theme of sex negotiating with money in the affair of Carrie and Drouet. This parallel between the sexual contest and the struggle for money must have a deeper source for Dreiser than the commercial culture's equation of everything with money; for when Hurstwood later tries for business success and fails, and fails to find or hold any sort of a job, Dreiser makes it clear that the major reason for this failure is not bad luck or social injustice but an inner failure of power, a deterioration that feeds on itself. It is true that Dreiser adds scenes that report on the marginal life of flophouses and soup kitchens and on a strike and its violence, but these provide only minor accents; they are part of the struggle for existence, though the roots are there for the politics that Dreiser later cultivated.

These reductive images of success and failure, of power as the abstraction behind the abstraction of success, all focus on the basic theme that life is a struggle. When Drouet is about to lose Carrie, he is described as like the emperor of China, unaware that his fairest provinces are being wrested from him. When Carrie begins to feel some alienation from him, the first effect is to make us see him as weak. This is a brief forecast of the more important later process of her being weaned from Hurstwood, where everything that happens accents his deterioration, and his weakness increases to the point where it would seem to the reader a totally ungrounded sacrifice for Carrie to stay with him. Dreiser manages this effect (and avoids any possible moral reproach for Carrie) by citing the decay of every faculty in Hurstwood, including even the capacity to feel hurt by her departure. His state is one of almost catatonic apathy, anticipating his eventual numb suicide.

The suicide scene illustrates the characteristic emotional flatness of naturalist fiction, the result of subordinating response to the movement of forces. For "the forces" do not simply overwhelm the capacity of a human character to define himself against them; rather, they *seem* to oppose themselves to a human interest but are then discovered to be the same as the natural process that determined the character's motive in the first place and then obstructed it. In other words, nature has its fifth column within every human organism. There is no contest in the last resort, as when, in Hurstwood's case, the blows of fate not only crush his strength but undermine his capacity to feel anything at all. The scenes describing his decline are perhaps the strongest in the novel; these are moments when naturalism seems to suggest its tragic possibilities and its authentic relation to biological fate. Perhaps *Sister Carrie* would have achieved tragic significance if Hurstwood had been given a more than rudimentary capacity for either thought or emotion. But how could he be given that when he has been described as a dying limb of life's organism, suffering a sort of self-amputation?

All the forces in Hurstwood's life are thus drawn into a single symbolic force. Dreiser has no interest in separate and opposite traits, as when a character might illustrate failure in one respect and continuing potency in another. Carrie, for instance, stops sleeping with Hurstwood when he manifests his decay of will and strength in his business ventures, but it appears that he himself loses interest in sex at the same time. The principle is illustrated with singular clarity in later fiction in the naturalist tradition, in the work of Hemingway, for instance, and, with even more emphasis, in that of Henry Miller and Norman Mailer, where competence in sex or in fighting is linked to a generalized potency to be found also in art, sport, politics, and other areas in which power may be sublimated.

This monistic theme of power suggests that a man is on the mark, to be tested by nature, and that he can be utterly condemned or glorified. It is a question of salvation, really, or sometimes resurrection, as in the case of Francis Macomber in Hemingway's most complete parable of normative naturalism. When Hurstwood fails, his failure covers him like an infection, and he begins to look repulsive to Carrie. What she is brought to feel is plausible, and there is no need to question the tough psychological realism of Dreiser's treatment. But its wholesale effect—its lack of modification or struggle, certainly the lack of guilt on one side or even hurt on the other—declares a complete subordination of the human sensibility to the power process. Is this stoic acknowledgment or superstitious respect for natural potency? It is hard to tell, both here and in other naturalist writing; but the latter effect is the stronger one at the end of Dreiser's novel.

An English critic, John Fraser, quotes and endorses a general comment on American movies: "There is no ruling class here, only a Darwinian struggle that divvies up Americans into winners and losers."[5] But the movies here referred to simply reflect something that is widespread in popular writing and conversation, where people are defined as "winners" or "losers," as if branded by a mark on their foreheads. Dreiser's novel shares in this superstition, if only because it is in essence a part of the naturalist myth, with its extraordinary focus on the totalist concept of force. Character does not have several departments of need and gratification, such as family happiness, status, wealth, love, and comfort. All inter-penetrate and affect one another, and pleasure cannot exist apart from their possession. Money and sex, particularly, are never sepa-rated; the possession of one makes possible the other, and both are linked with status and success.

The point of focus for Dreiser was, obviously, the competition for wealth in a capitalist culture and the assumption that you can buy anything with money and can have nothing without it. How-ever, by the strength of his art, he creates a larger myth of power in which wealth is only the instrument of the struggle for survival and the means for making the most of biological destiny. Its possession is the sign that one has gained and maintained the maximum potency of natural being. Its loss, as well as the loss of sexual power, can mean something metaphysical in the end, as drastic as a doom from heaven.

Passivity and Violence

Carrie, in her first relations with Drouet and Hurstwood, does not choose: she surrenders, they conquer. The passage between Drouet and Carrie implies a sexual contest, but the intention is actually to stress victimization and entrapment, both of which fea-ture the weight of external or environmental "forces." Carrie has a minimal passionate involvement with both men, though Hurst-wood has a stronger effect on her imagination. The theme for her action is "she could not resist," and, even when she has feeling, it seems only to mirror the stronger feelings of the men. In retro-spect, the reader asks, why should she resist, and, if she does, with what force should she do so? It is made clear that Carrie is affected hardly at all by conventional prohibitions. As for a sense of danger to herself or to her real interests, it is quickly made evident that her life after her seduction is quite comfortable and even enjoyable, a great step beyond factory work and the grim life with her sister.

Resistance seems to be set up as an essential part of the sexual struggle: the woman resists as a matter of nature—almost, it seems, as if to invite male aggression. If she did not resist, she could not subsequently submit, and the male would be deprived of part of his sexual pleasure, which is conquest. This theme is clearest in the writing of Frank Norris, since his view of sexuality is closer to vitalism than Dreiser's, which remains sociologically oriented. In

McTeague the courtship of Trina is marked by McTeague's animal awkwardness until he blunders into an embrace:

> He had only to take her in his arms, to crush down her struggle with his enormous strength, to subdue her, conquer her by sheer brute force, and she gave up in an instant. [*Mc* 65]

Nothing quite like this happens in *Sister Carrie,* though as an expression of what might be called the folkways of seduction Carrie offers Hurstwood the passivity the male desires and imposes on women: she is "the victim of his keen eyes, his suave manners, his fine clothes...answering vaguely, languishing affectionately, and altogether drifting" (*SC* 171). There is pleasure in "drifting," but that sort of submission is not all the emphasis that Dreiser wants. Carrie is finally trapped by the deception with which Hurstwood gets her onto the train to Detroit. And when Hurstwood discloses his lie, as he must when the train gathers distance from Chicago, the possibility of getting off the train is put out of Carrie's mind by the late hour, the rain outside, and by her rather infantile desire to see Montreal and other distant places while she has the chance. Infantile is the right word for this sort of passivity, for submission to external force and deception emphasizes helplessness, fear, and reflexive or dependent emotions. Thus Carrie, at the point of surrender, though impressed by the supposed power of Hurstwood's emotion ("her resistance half dissolved in the flood of his strong feeling") must ask herself, "Where else might she go? . . . He loved her, and she was alone" (*SC* 235). It is relevant to make the point that vulnerability, passivity, and dependent infantilism are all traits brought into the foreground by the deterministic sociology of force and frequently exploited in the naturalist politics of the "masses." The historical and cultural significance of naturalist fiction is suggested by the firm outline Dreiser gives to Carrie's need, her drifting or unfocused capacity to choose, and the web of circumstance that encloses Hurstwood as well as herself.

To stress the comprehensiveness of his view of motivation, Dreiser does not restrict passivity and infantilism to a dependent female, for Hurstwood makes the fundamental decision of his life in an essentially similar fashion. By the time he confronts the safe in his office containing the money he needs for escaping with Carrie, his external situation has reached a climax of frustration. Frustration is the keynote; and just as submission to external force characterizes Carrie, Hurstwood's attention is focused on the circumstances that block his way. It is almost as if Dreiser had forgotten to give play to the passion Hurstwood feels for Carrie, the inner drive that brings him to his predicament; we seem to know of his desire chiefly from the obstacles that stand in its way: his wife's control over his money, his employers' objection to divorce or scandal, Carrie's discovery of his marriage, and his absolute need for cash to finance his escape. These dominate his mind not only in this crucial scene but in the preparation for it. But to make sure that the reader does not look too closely for ordinary moral responsibility, Dreiser gives the final momentum to simple accident. Hurstwood has taken the money out of the safe, as if only to look at it desirefully, but the door clicks shut. Not knowing the combination, he is now condemned to making an embarrassing explanation the next morning, since his job, though he is the manager, has nothing to do with handling cash. The fatalism of chance is necessary to the stress on drift and dependency; no free agent can rival process here.[6] Indecision here does not indicate a struggle between the power of moral resistance and the force of temptation but rather a kind of personal stalemate, as Hurstwood, like Carrie, is manipulated almost helplessly in a field of forces both major and minor. Did the rainy weather that night in Detroit determine Carrie's future? It is impossible to give a simple yes to that, but both the rain and the force of gravity that swung the safe door shut are meant to weigh more than clear value choices, and of course the author excludes conscience entirely: "The true ethics of the situation never once occurred to him, and never would have, under any circumstances" (*SC* 221). Why this should be so is not really clear, and the dismissal of "ethics" seems quite as theoretical and arbitrary as a conventional moralism would be. Conscience disappears into a primitive and simple fear of the police when Hurstwood recognizes, after he is on the train, that "They would be after him" (*SC* 221).

However, this view of character as dominated almost exclusively by external forces and lacking an inner life makes possible the impressive exhibition of Hurstwood's decline as status and wealth desert him. Dreiser has drawn him from the beginning as a man of externals, taking his character from his job, where he functions as a hand-shaker with the mission of pleasing others, particularly the rich and successful. That this is all he is, or was, is conclusively demonstrated by the fact that hardly a trace of feeling in Carrie survives Hurstwood's progressive loss of job, money, and public status. It is a mistake, however, to regard this as reductively cold and unfeeling, for what the author is emphasizing is the public or social nature of suffering. That shadow of a man, Hurstwood, appeals to an essentially political concern. Externalized in his wealth and prosperity, empty entirely in his misfortunes, he may be intended for the care of social doctors who might replace one lost exoskeleton of identity with another.

Taking this view of character as controlled and automatistic, it would be easy for a behaviorist engineer to manipulate circumstances in Hurstwood's life to gain a different result, since Hurstwood himself is so amenable to arrangement. Offering his own naturalist premise in the text, Dreiser remarks that man was once naturally and successfully an animal and that now his whole purpose must be to function as smoothly again, by "learning" what nature once gave without instruction:

> As a beast, the forces of life aligned him with them; as a man, he has not yet wholly learned to align himself with the forces. [SC 67]

This absurd "evolutionary" development gives the intelligence, together with all of its civilized instruments, the paradoxical task of returning its owner to a happier original alignment with nature. A vitalist naturalism would more plausibly conceive that a harmony of this kind is better achieved through the instincts; the function of the authorial intelligence would then be not to map alignments with nature but to force them through deep penetrations of passion and instinct. However, since Dreiser gave the greater role to outward conditioning, there is in his work the accent on passivity that usually goes with a strong mechanistic emphasis. What should interest a student of naturalist fiction in general is the marked alternations between mechanistic and vitalist effects that occur, sometimes in the same work, with a large web of circumstances controlling action in one scene and explosive passion erupting in another.

Norris's writing makes this dualism of effect more directly evident. In *The Octopus,* Shelgrim, the corporate leader of the railroad, sums up the impersonality of power thus: *"Railroads build themselves....* Men have only little to do in the whole business.... Blame conditions, not men."[7] The temptation to passivity is evident, but the deeper temptation may be to identify with some "force," otherwise uncontrollable—to let it act *through* oneself and to profit by it, as Shelgrim surely does, though he says, "I can *not* control it. It is a force [and] I—no man—can stop it or control it" (*O* 396). Beyond surrender or manipulation there is the alternative of blind resistance, like that of the violent Dyke, who in Norris's novel is maddened to the point of participating in the destruction of his farm, his family, and himself.

What is important to note is the context of violence. When power is the measure and the multitude of men and women are found to be relatively impotent in the face of events and circumstances, it is almost inevitable that reactive violence *should* be the one alternative to the usual passivity. A desperate impulse to resist, like Dyke's, must lead to failure, but it points to the more promising possibility of collective resistance. Collective violence in many naturalist novels, like the streetcar strike in *Sister Carrie* or the ranchers' demonstrations in *The Octopus,* must be seen in the context of the dominant role assigned to social forces, like the Railroad or the impersonal City, and the helplessness assigned to individual protagonists. Given the drifting submission of most of the characters and the isolated self-destructive outbreaks of a few, the conditions are set up for socially meaningful and possibly effective violence through collective action. This requires no political ideology for its discovery. The conclusion seems inevitable from the premise that men are ruled by forces in conflict; for if this is true, the best way to avoid being the victim of a social force is to identify with it, and the only way to oppose one social force is to take sides with another.

Victimization and Resentment

Stephen Crane's writing lacks the impressive documentation whose enormous weight finally gives Dreiser's work an effect appropriately related to the awe Henry Adams felt before the Dynamo. But Crane comes closer to revealing the impact of violence, for he presents the naturalist laws of conflict and victimization with such clarity that the reader knows, with some relief, that he is in the presence of a literary myth and not the hybrid product of literature, social science, and political ideology that is so often found in conventional naturalist fiction.

In Crane's *Maggie,* for instance, the boys fighting in the streets assume the bearing of "one who aimed to be some vague soldier, or a man of blood."[8] Pete is the "supreme warrior," and Maggie is helplessly attracted to him by the prowess of his fists, his fine clothing, and his contempt for the rest of the world. The city street is the scene of life's struggle, and Maggie's brother, Jimmie, forms himself in its image. "In revenge, he resolved never to move out of the way of anything, until formidable circumstances, or a much larger man than himself forced him to it" (*Ma* 15). Once Jimmie has learned to respect only the fire engine, the symbol of superior force ("an appalling thing that he loved with . . . dog-like devotion" [*Ma* 16]) his relations with the rest of the world must become conflict-oriented, and he typically adapts to the world with the manifestations of a paranoid personality. This response is grounded as firmly in his origins as though he had grown up with dangerous wildlife in the woods. His mother, a monstrous creature of malice, could look at Jimmie with an expression that "had the power to change his blood to salt" (*Ma* 12). But the street was Jimmie's primary teacher, "a world full of fists," dominated only by the fire engine and, at times, the police.[9]

> To him the police were always actuated by malignant impulses and the rest of the world was composed, for the most part, of despicable creatures who were all trying to take advantage of him and with whom, in defence, he was obliged to quarrel on all possible occasions. [*Ma* 14]

Crane's constant stress on defensive belligerence in Pete and Jimmie, the street warriors, is paralleled by the pathos of Maggie's complete victimization. A superior force can arouse fear in victims but also, in the right context, the "dog-like devotion" that Maggie feels for Pete: "To her the earth was composed of hardship and insults. She felt instant admiration for a man who openly defied it" (*Ma* 20). She herself has no capacity for resistance or defiance, and Crane uses the pathos of her situation to add emotional appeal to naturalist conflict. As the victim she makes a poignant contrast with strength and in doing so provides the sentiment that is usually a part of the cult of power. She is described, for instance, as a girl blossoming in a mud puddle: "None of the dirt of Rum Alley seemed to be in her veins" (*Ma* 16). Her chief role is to suffer and to dream, with dim thoughts of "dream gardens" and a lover and faraway lands where "the little hills sing together in the morning" (*Ma* 19). The aim of the plot is to sacrifice this innate refinement to the coarse violence of the streets. As a woman, Maggie is the virginal sacrifice to Pete's warrior pride and lust. But to compound the victimization, she is also the child, remaining as she was, early in the story, where she and Jimmie are described as two children huddling together in a world full of savage animals. She is also as deluded as a child because she is capable of imagining Pete as a man of the world, a cultured gentleman. This is excessive irony on Crane's part, but it is symptomatic of the patronizing sentiment that was strongly characteristic of early naturalist fiction, where the people for whom the reader can be asked to feel sympathy are so often as dependent and vulnerable as children. The pathos of weakness is linked to a bias on behalf of the "oppressed," and this becomes visibly related to the fuller development of naturalist politics.

Characters so helplessly abused as Maggie are meant to arouse a sympathy based on the fact of their being doubly victimized by society. Maggie is first of all the victim of the street anarchy and the specifically sexual competition of street warriors like Pete, who considers her his natural victim, as Jimmie would, too, if she weren't his sister. This point is sharply made because Jimmie and their savage mother are the agents of the punishment that Maggie suffers for her sexual fall. When they throw her out to her final destruction as "a girl of the streets," they are asserting a moral standard in grotesque disharmony with their own behavior. Crane is not so concerned with the specific plausibility of this as he is in stressing that his victim is doubly oppressed: by the violence of the slum, where people are brought to the edge of savagery, and also, if contradictorily, by the repressive social forces that define wrong behavior and punish it.

The link in naturalist thought to large issues is suggested by one critic, Donald Pizer. Justly pointing out that Crane's characters exhibit "a core of animality and a shell of moral poses," Pizer, like many readers of naturalist fiction, devotes most of his attention to the "shell," that is, to the hypocrisy inherent in the system of middle-class morality. It is true that one is faced with an interesting complexity in trying to decide which is Maggie's greater enemy, the jungle life of sexual exploitation or the social persecution that comes later. As Pizer reads him, Crane is working with the double theme that men cannot control their destinies, which are determined by environmental and instinctual forces, but that they can, at least, destroy those systems of value that uncritically pretend to control naturalist fate. "If we do this [i.e., destroy these systems of value], a Maggie (or a Jennie Gerhardt) will at least be saved from condemnation and destruction by an unjust code."[10]

Here I think Pizer is reflecting accurately an ambivalence at the heart of naturalist writing, in which those who are powerless—the victims of either natural or social forces—are revenged when the writer attacks moral conventions as illusions or hypocrisy. The resentment of the victims, aroused by amoral biological or social fate, can be converted into a war against bourgeois morality. In *Maggie,* a youthful work, written in an age of muckraking and social reform, Crane was undoubtedly responding to deep currents of popular thought, in which society's laws are seen to oppress people, particularly the poor, and the police are dramatized as the enemy of those who are in fact society's victims. More oppressive than the police are the conventional moral stereotypes, which are embodied even in such wretched degenerates as Maggie's mother and the tough saloonkeeper who abuses Maggie and ejects her from his place. By a curious but typical maneuver, the sexual anarchy that abuses Maggie is made to seem the ally of the moral system that punishes illicit behavior.

Intensely conceived naturalist fiction like Crane's enables us to
see the almost simultaneous action of two kinds of moral criticism:
people are viewed as victims of repressive social standards, and
they are seen as the victims of nature's violence. A moralizing naturalist writer tends often to link these two forms of oppression.[11]
The more ideological fiction of Dos Passos illustrates the point by
its repeated use of the effect of cumulative victimization and injury
from both nature and society.

Many of the characters in Dos Passos's *USA*, for instance, begin
their adult lives by experiencing sex traumas, which form their
characters and seem to form even their political attitudes. There is
the case of Janey, who in an early sexual experience weeps but
thereafter reacts with "cold, hard feeling" when things upset her.
Her defensive shallowness seems to be the basis of her later loyalty
to her boss, Ward Moorehouse, and her coldness toward her
unionizing brother, Joe. Moorehouse is a caricature of the
businessman-opportunist, incapable of honest feeling, for he, too,
like Janey, has been the victim of early disillusionment: he was
trapped by his promiscuous first wife, Annabelle, into marriage
after a sexual encounter. He and his later mistress, Eleanor Stoddard, a snobbish social climber, are partners in a worldly alliance,
lacking passion of any kind. The sexuality of Barrow, the union
leader who sells out labor, has become lecherous and dirty—"his
eyes got a watery look."[12] In contrast, respectable "puritan" re-
straints are despised, even while sexual selfishness, cruelty, in-
fidelity, and abuse are made the basis of lifelong trauma. Ward
Moorehouse was sexually sentimental before being seduced by
Annabelle, who is pregnant with another man's child. He "was
twenty and didn't drink or smoke and was keeping himself clean
for the lovely girl he was going to marry, a girl in pink organdy with
golden curls and a sunshade" (*USA* 117).

Such illusions are meretricious; they represent a false social system and its standards. But truth is a rough taskmaster, and the
truth of nature can be as ruthless to emancipated sensibilities as to
those protected by conventional pieties. Dos Passos was obsessed by
the rapacity of sexual appetites and the cold law of sexual competition, but it is not the violence of nature alone that touches his
characteristic sensitivity. The naturalist portrayal of human life as
subject to the casual drift of animal appetite and instinct could lead
finally to the wholesale trivialization of existence. In this respect, as
well as in his attention to the naturalist shock of violence, Dos
Passos belongs to his own generation, that of Hemingway and
Nathanael West. In all of these writers moral indignation is
undermined and seemingly canceled by a philosophic defeatism,

or, conversely, metaphysical outrage is added to legitimate social and cultural criticism.

The important hypothesis here is that a revulsion against biological fate, though rarely overt, is often covert in naturalist fiction and that a resentment bred by it can find its target in society, the established culture, and, of course, in politics. A clear illustration of this, I have suggested, can be found in the naturalist writers' treatment of sexual conflict in the context of a commercial society. Writers who show Marxist inclinations, like Dos Passos (in *USA*) and Dreiser, can treat sex as part of a system of exploitation: women trap men, men buy women. Sexual conflict is thus linked with competition for money; sex and money are both free-market exchanges of strength, and there is no mercy for the weak or the sentimentally deluded. But sex is at the same time presented as a deeper threat, as a form of primitive biological exploitation; it thus serves to join the injustice of society to the deeper injustice of nature.

Another example of a covert metaphysical despair that turns on society in revenge can be found in the naturalists' treatment of war, a theme that occupied so prominent a place in the works of Dos Passos and Hemingway and their contemporaries. War could be viewed (and was so viewed by Crane in *The Red Badge of Courage*) as the human form of Darwinian conflict, the competition between species becoming conflict between human groups. But in Dos Passos and others war is seen less as the outcome of primordial natural competition and more as a vice of civilization. It is not instinctive violence that dominates in this view of war but a kind of corrupt ethics called patriotism.[13] This violence, then, is inspired by a false value, a mendacious faith. Self-interest is, of course, the strong motive behind the patriotic bloodlust of cold, aggrandizing characters like Moorehouse and Eleanor, but it is a form of self-interest that no longer appears natural, i.e., Darwinian, but one bred and sanctioned by a social system. The war profiteers and careerists, the manipulators and opportunists, are all so deeply embedded in a system of illusory values and lies that the violence of the Darwinian principle of competition, or even the simple inevitabilities of physical suffering and death, have all been absorbed by a resentment directed against national and cultural ideologies.

Thus the war conflict, like the sex conflict, in Dos Passos's work (and in Hemingway's *A Farewell to Arms*) adds naturalist shock to revolutionary protest. The sum is a powerful double indictment, giving a political meaning to what might otherwise be considered universal, natural, and inevitable human suffering. The point is not that political meanings are invalid, particularly in the social conflict of wars; it is rather that these writers have piled the sum of human rage and frustration on the back of the political beast the way Ahab piled his on the White Whale. This may help to explain the historical success achieved by naturalist politics, in which a possibly nihilistic but essentially subversive hostility is transferred from nature, as the ultimate oppressor, to society or culture. Culture suffers the revenge of the deprived; failing to maintain faith in itself, accused of lying from the start in its assertion of ethical authority, as well as in its original claim to be linked with nature through an ominipotent God, it becomes the easiest target of contempt and rage. Its authority must be unmasked, not just because it is based on falsehood but because it can give no real protection from the greater enemy, nature itself. The intransigence of revolutionary doctrine in our era may be understood in the context of this great unsatisfied demand on society to protect human life from natural process or to rediscover an old harmony that promised safety and fulfillment.

The revolutionary implications of naturalist literature were clearly voiced from the start, mixed, as always, with impulses of revenge and hope. Zola declared the political force of his literary doctrine and foresaw the literary triumph of naturalism as coinciding with the victory of "the Republic, which is now in process of being established by science and reason."[14] In this he was the prophet of hope. But he understood, he said, why his enemies dragged him in the mud: "I quite see the reason. It is because we deny their *bon Dieu*, we empty their heaven, we take no account of the ideal, we do not refer everything to that abstraction."[15] And although Zola seriously claimed to emulate science in his pursuit of the truth, other reflections of his indicate that, when it came to "reality," the naturalist could be very selective and that his overriding interest was to destroy false idealizations. Guy de Maupassant was blunt in saying that, "When you look at it closely, the persistent representation of 'lower elements' is, in fact, only a protest against adherence to a poetical view of things."[16] In this he spoke for a revenging truth of fiction and science whose plain mission was to sweep the world of lies.

Revenge is really the only adequate word for describing the reflexive hatred of idealizations one finds in the naturalist literary tradition and in that branch of "modernism" most affected by it. In Europe, writers like Strindberg and Artaud come to mind. Malcolm Cowley noted early the penchant for self-injury in the writing of the American naturalists. He concluded that in this respect American naturalists were neither cynics nor realists but men who had been morally wounded and were flaunting their wounds in their writing. Intrinsically, Cowley says, the sense of moral fitness is strong in them; they believe in their hearts that nature *should* be kind, that virtue *should* be rewarded on earth, that men *should* control their own destinies . . .; they often give the impression of seeking out ugliness and injustice in order to be wounded again and again . . . . They seem to be flogging themselves and their audience like a band of penitentes.[17]

This insight lays bare the profound emotional dialectic that inhabits the spirit of both naturalist fiction and naturalist politics, a dialectic in which injury from nature becomes injury from society. In its own revolutionary commitment, Marxism illustrates the double alienation expressed in naturalist fiction. Capitalist society and all human history exhibit the law of naturalist conflict, the struggle between classes developing from the basic competition for survival. The real intention of naturalist politics is not to justify the law of dialectical conflict (though in theory a Marxist would deny any intention to arrest the essential law of history) but to lead conflict toward its only possible resolution, one that grows out of natural and historical process. Acceptance of nature's law is transferred from stoic endurance to hope, and that political hope is paradoxically based on moral revulsion from the economic law of the survival of the fittest and, one might say, from the general view of nature as a gigantic and universal system of exploitation. Thus the fervor of naturalist politics is inspired by its implied mastery over both social laws and natural forces (since its doctrine springs from the understanding of both social and natural forces) and by its ability to pose as the champion of man against both antagonists, sometimes alternately and sometimes both at once. The comprehensive effect of revolutionary naturalist politics is to make a brilliant resolution of the conflict between nature and society, lifting the oppressive weight of both from man. It can seem to satisfy two rival needs, emphasizing liberation in the first phase of the revolutionary cycle, as if to set nature free from the burden of culture; but then, with the second phase, it promises a new social order, one that will subdue the least threat of natural anarchy. The miracle is the frequent ability of a revolutionary program to promise both liberation and a new discipline at the same time.

Naturalist Fiction and Political Allegory

In *Sister Carrie,* Hurstwood's decline is played out against a background of social struggle; during a motorman's strike he works as a scab and is almost killed in street violence. Later he sinks into marginal survival in flophouses and soup kitchens. The fading of

Hurstwood's personal power, the deterioration of all his faculties, supports the transfer of attention to the social issue. As the possibility of self-redemption or even personal enlightenment is canceled out, a moral responsibility is being offered to society. Nothing can be done for Hurstwood as an individual, and he can do nothing for himself; but that perception is a way of enforcing the shift of moral responsibility from particulars to universals, from individuals to groups. Biological fate dictates the short cycles of individual life and death, strength and the fading of strength, but for the species there is a recourse from this fate. Thus, all that is lost in the life of individuals—the possibility of purpose, the possibility of redemption—can be subsumed into history and into the effort to direct history through political action.

This is a way of defining the important role of politics in naturalist fiction. One imagines that the first requirement of a determinist politics is to propose the existence of victims whose helplessness simulates the conditions of the experimental laboratory Zola held up as the model for fiction. There is a great deal of melodramatic sentiment in an episode of Norris's *The Octopus* that describes the total victimization of the Hooven family through a series of misfortunes, beginning with the dazed confusion of an immigrant German farmer and ending with his violent death, the prostitution of his daughter, and the death through starvation of Mrs. Hooven on the streets of San Francisco. But no specific moral monster—no person—can be held responsible for these outrages. The sequence is set off by the selfish imperial power of the Railroad, but, once it starts, fortuitous accidents appear to play a strong role, as when Mrs. Hooven's note, directing Minna where to find her, is lost. It becomes evident, however, that these "accidents" are due to the inscrutable operation of "Forces" massed against human beings and their powerless hopes and needs. Since these Forces partake of the metaphysical, resistance to them, if any is possible, must operate on the same level. Thus moral or political programs assume the same features—equally abstract and impersonal and with equal authority—as historic fate.

In Norris's work this idea is used almost as a formula for the presentation of ethical sentiments and judgments. A shocking extremity of suffering is visited on an extremely vulnerable person, and both the suffering and the vulnerability are the products of the impersonal movement of "forces." Ethical outrage is thus pitted against a nonethical power, and the resulting dramatic effects are the most significant ones in the story.[18] For instance, Magnus Derrick and his rancher friends go to great lengths to put his son Lyman into a position of political power in the contest between the wheat-growers and the railroad corporation. They realize that they must do as the Railroad does, and so Lyman's election is won through political bribery. The aristocratic Magnus Derrick feels trapped and humiliated by this imitation of the vulgar power plays of his enemies, but the helplessness of this sentiment is illustrated when his son, himself bribed with the promise of great wealth and power, turns against his father and sells him out. Our horror at this betrayal is not undermined by the author's neutral view of overwhelming forces pitted against the feeble, subjective ethics of men. Neutrality and cynicism are possible reactions, but the response dictated by the author, even if it is masked by objective detachment, remains one of moral outrage. Thus the naturalist view retains its moral bias even as it presents an impersonal estimate of the enemy's power and a cold determination to wield an equal power.

Therefore, when Norris has Shelgrim, the Railroad leader, say "Blame conditions, not men," and "I can *not* control it. It is a Force," the effect is not necessarily one of submission to fate. What must be sought is a counterforce, equally inscrutable, equally the product of "conditions, not men." Norris finds this in the vitalist force of the Wheat, stronger than machines and money and, in effect, the guardian of the real interest of men, which is their share in the vitalist process. Meanwhile, if an interest is at stake or an outrage is to be revenged, the needed superior force can be brought into play if men are transformed, allegorized, into "conditions." Behrman, the active Railroad manager on the scene, is allegorized in this way. He is finally extinguished by suffocation in an ocean of wheat, poured into the hold of the ship, where he has been trapped. And, most welcome of all, no human agent has exacted this punishment. It is an accident, or rather a "condition," as if the Wheat itself had decided finally to punish Behrman, the agent of the Railroad.

Behrman's role is representative of the process of political abstraction—a process that Norris, in the eagerness of his convictions, was one of the first to emphasize in American naturalist fiction. Dos Passos, in a documentary vein that contrasts with Norris's melodrama, indicates again how naturalist fiction adapts to political allegory. The programmatic effect of Dos Passos's *USA* trilogy is the complete subordination of individual lives to the historic social process. Public life so overwhelms private life that the fragments of lives we are presented with in Janey and Joe, Moorehouse and Eleanor, seem only illustrative footnotes to large events. The "Headlines" supply a drama that is almost entirely missing in the narrative. In effect the reader is told to go to the "Newsreel" sections of the text for the real story; it is the public themes, essentially political, that determine what is significant. The result, of course, is to lean on political ideology, to let general patterns of judgment interpret these lives for us. And in an even more suggestive link with naturalist politics, the passivity of most people—the ordinary, everyday people—in *USA* opens up the distinctive role given to the leaders and inventors, the manipulators of things and persons, who are featured in the "Biographies" that regularly interrupt the narrative text. The general run of characters are pressed into the roles of average victim or average opportunist and profit-maker. Their lives are tedious and routine; there are no large moments, no charged excitements, even on a personal level. In contrast, the "Biography" sections feature heroes or villains like Eugene Debs, Big Bill Haywood, Henry Ford, J. Pierpont Morgan—each a public monument who casts a giant shadow. These strong characters may be as much identified with social "forces" as the little people, but they are separated from the mass because of their strength, their vividness, their real effect on the social process. These people manipulate and handle power, but their motives are inaccessible, their humanity minimal, perhaps because images of power tend to leave such terms behind. In combination with the army of small characters, they feed the paranoid tendencies of the political imagination, the world divided between men of great power and the people of the mass, who are singled out, if at all, for their representative qualities or else, as the occasion demands, for the pathos of their suffering.[19]

The author's distinctions between good and bad people are obvious in the contrast he draws between public characters like Bill Haywood and Henry Ford, but the miniature characters are also categorized. Thus Janey, though not as sympathetic as her working-stiff brother Joe, is a loyal and forlorn stenographer, the conventionally burdened female, with definite limits placed on her life. Above her on the social scale, Eleanor Stoddard is an egotistical snob, striving to move to higher class and cultural levels and rendered emotionally frigid by her ambition and struggle for money. Though she becomes a manipulator of esthetic values, these have been made shallow and pretentious not by her character but by her context: the way of life and social psychology she is supposed to illustrate. It is a blameworthy way of life—or so we can judge when Eleanor accepts money from her working-class father while hating him and promising herself never to see him again. There is not much reason for her hostility except for the aura of low beginnings that clings to him. When she finally allies herself with Moorehouse, we can expect any sort of rottenness from both of them. But their evil is quite impersonal and dehumanized. The prejudice against them, communicated to the reader, is abstract and as class-oriented as Eleanor's own revulsion from her father.

This moral thinness of character is a weak dramatic basis for presenting human relationships; the social pattern is obviously strong and determining, and yet there is watery response and very limited allegiance in the actual relationships we observe. In *USA* people move in and out of each other's lives without producing much effect; even those who are closest to each other, like Janey and her brother Joe, seem absentminded when they meet again. Joe and Mac leave home as young men almost as a matter of course, feeling not the vaguest homesickness or yearning for something lost. Transient lovers like Annabelle and Moorehouse or Janey and Burnham illustrate a general principle: people come close, engage, and then drift apart.

All this might be described as the accurate report of a decadent, disheartened society, and so I believe it was taken by most readers in their first response to it. But considered judgment suggests that these effects are the product of an abstract political vision, one that tells us that generalized social forces and simple natural instincts dominate people's lives. In that view, survival is the most important of motives, and, following from that, the range of motivations is severely limited. There is the need for money; there is social ambition—that is, the struggle for power and status; and there is sex. Beyond that, or, rather, draped over them for concealment, there remains the pseudo-ethic of conventional respectability. The formula is a familiar one and central to the myth of naturalism. Values are fictions, instincts are real, behavior is selfish. A typical tradeoff is the one that takes place between Moorehouse and Annabelle, his first wife, after the early wounding of his young and conventional sexual idealism (one siege of weeping and he becomes an opportunist again). Basically, they exchange for what they each need: Ward wants money and sex, Annabelle wants respectability—and sex. This barrenness of motive should dull the reader, and, if it doesn't, it is perhaps because the reductive simplicity is on a universal scale. There is, of course, the possibility of violent response in any sequence dealing with sex, and Dos Passos does not forget violence in the highly visible pattern of a naturalist myth of sex. The rule in such fiction is somewhat as follows: violence or erotic demonstrations will increase in proportion to the lack of psychological nuance and complexity of character. The simplest example is the violence that breaks from Norris's McTeague, as if in revolt from his own numb intelligence and inarticulateness. And, in Dos Passos, it is striking to see how often an erotic crisis or some personally experienced physical abuse is made to interrupt and season the massive sociological documentation. The effect in general terms is one of alternation between triviality and sensationalism. If the social documentation is boring, the naturalist novelist has a remedy available in the devices of melodramatic political allegory or in the "realism" of sexual shock and violence.

Both dramatic violence and the panorama of sociological abstraction are by-products of the naturalist's reductive view of character, but a more significant result is the spirit of condescension implicit in it. In naturalist fiction the poverty of the characters' responses is often conveyed by infantile simplicities of style, and, with sometimes powerful dramatic irony, this style is used to describe even the most serious and painful experiences. The dominant stylistic influences on Dos Passos were surely Hemingway, Stein, and Sherwood Anderson, although he lacks the intense stoic drama or poetic primitivism that enlivens their works. And, what is also more evident in Dos Passos's writing, the infantilism of style has the effect of emphasizing the infantile vulnerability of characters. The reader's moral sympathy must focus first on a generality of suffering, a social condition, and second on a mass dependency that begs for protection and direction.

The question arises, why did two or more generations of writers feel it necessary to diminish the moral size and personal strength and intelligence of their characters? Was it because they turned to ordinary people for their subjects? Was it because an oppressive and corrupt social system had reduced most people to these dimensions? Or was it the response to tendentious thinking about human nature based on social and biological naturalism? It is a bothersome question, seemingly reversible in terms of cause and effect, because it is affected by various uncontrolled factors. It may be that the bottom half of human society could never exhibit more than this narrow range of sensibility, having neither the opportunity nor the capacity for making meaningful choices. Therefore, a literature of the "people" must do what it can with such limitations and risk being reductive and patronizing, as a politics of the "people" will also risk forms of paternalist and authoritarian intervention. On the other hand, the limitation may be in the point of view, in which a simplified, empirical, reductive understanding of the typical case, the average human being, always produces distortions.

These allegorical effects of naturalism are pushed to an ideological extreme in Frank Norris's work, perhaps because, ambitious to write an American epic, he rightly understood that he was dealing with mythic substance. In *McTeague*, for instance, the struggle for money plays the central dramatic role, and it is doubtful that this is a response to the social reality that Norris knew best. Rather, it is a great and inclusive ordering principle, a surreal obsession that drives all the characters almost as blindly as it sweeps Zerkow, the miser, toward murder and self-destruction. Rival instincts and motives converge on this one point, greed, as when Marcus Schouler, after first accepting generously the loss of his girl, Trina, to McTeague, finds his friendship turning to jealous hatred when Trina wins a five-thousand-dollar lottery prize just before her marriage. Money is what cements and then divides her marriage, for Trina's new fortune, infecting her with greed, finally drives her husband to kill her. And when Schouler hunts McTeague to his death, his own greed for gold dominates his need for revenge, his hunter's sadism, and even his own instinct for survival.[20] This convergence of motives reaches an inventive climax when Norris shows Trina directly substituting money for sex: in a climax of miserly pleasures, she pours her gold onto her bed, undresses, and sleeps naked with it.

What Norris has done is to fuse biological and social abstractions of force, pour them into the same mold, and, in doing so, reach the point where social conflicts take on the metaphysical character of biological process and naturalist fate. To think of social and economic relations in such terms is to mythologize them and make them absolute. We see McTeague and Schouler magnified in that kind of metaphysical drama as they wrestle to their deaths even when they know they are already doomed by the desert and the loss of their supply of water. It is as if life cannot be allowed to end on any accent but violence. In this novel's context (which is intellectually based on the abstraction of economic conflict), Zerkow's murderous greed, Trina's miserliness, and Schouler's revenge are not strange pathologies; they are simple representations of the strongest force ruling behavior, the demon that drives history. If interpreted in a political spirit, what counterforce would not be justified in the effort to master it?

The allegory of "forces" in literary naturalism leads plausibly to the allegory of groups. There was sanction for this, it seemed, from Darwin; and if McTeague is large and violent on the scene, fighting for his survival, how much larger and more violent would the struggle be if it were not just for himself but for his species? Norris is a man of his intellectual period in the way he thrusts racial concepts and group stereotypes into the foreground of attention. In *The Octopus* the degenerate mixed-breed Spanish of California love the cruelty of the great rabbit slaughter, a kind of epitome of the novel's extended violence. The supreme villain, Behrman, is "Hebraic," cautious and scheming, as much without mercy as the Jew Zerkow in *McTeague*. Lyman Derrick, the renegade son, is described as having a dark face and popeyes, and it is repeatedly emphasized that he is foreign-looking. For contrast, we have sturdy Americans endowed with fair Anglo-Saxon strength and beauty.

If the hints of racism are strong in *The Octopus*, it is because Norris is dealing ultimately with "forces, not men," and so, appropriately, he will see groups when he treats of individuals. The crude stereotypes of race do not generally lend themselves to fiction, but the roots of racist judgment and feeling are present in the initial stereotypes of the forces that motivate men and rule life. Thus Behrman illustrates a mean lust for power, but Magnus Derrick represents the power drive absorbed in a generous and aristocratic, though fallible, principle of leadership. Such human divisions are easy to make and tempting. Vanamee represents the spiritual man, Presley, the man of conscience and poetry, and Annixter, to complete the triad of young protagonists, the virile man, dominated by physical action and the love of work. The women are even more distinctively classified. Hilda, representing vital sex, is linked with the earth and the wheat, while Angéle, also a spirit in nature, meets Vanamee's more intense and transcendental aspirations. Adams's Venus-Virgin figure is here divided into its components, but both are representations of energy, attracting and endowing the men. And the men, even the sympathetic figures, are accordingly dedicated to controlling some form of power. Vanamee, the mystic, wishes to control ultimate, supernatural forces; Presley, the poet, wishes to master experience and all its meanings; while Annixter, the man of action, wants to control the land and the wheat. The rest of the characters are driven in the same direction, though on more prosaic levels, preoccupied as they are with the direct objectives of economic and political power.

Such one-dimensional characters take their interest from the naturalist value conflicts they exhibit. In other words, they function as allegorical figures in a myth. Some exhibit positive vitalism, like Hilma and Annixter, while others represent the "soulless force," the ironhearted power of the Machine. The Machine, and the abstract power of money behind it, almost visibly compel Norris to elaborate the rival vitalist powers found in the Woman, the Wheat, and the People. (All such "forces" need capitalization, in Norris's view.) We sense the presence of another vitalist god in Race, though it does not receive the same explicit treatment. But a symbol that does link group forces comes forward in the idea of Empire. The work of Henry Adams suggests that the nineteenth-century cults of race and empire were vitalist, intended to rival the supremacy of science, technology, and finance, purging them of their dehumanizing implications. Norris exhibits the same response, paralleling Adams more clearly than any other naturalist fiction writer. In writing of the "great West," he calls up epic effects. It is the promise of empire, "vast . . . vaster . . . immensities multiplying," that inspires Presley with "stupendous ideas for which there were no names," and the "vast terrible song" he hears he calls the "Song of the People," though it is at the same time the song of Empire (*O* 33, 29). For Presley, the poet, these are gods: "The voice of God is the voice of the People," he says in his enthusiasm, and Norris writes, "He *believed* and so to him all things were possible at once" (*O* 377, 255).

The main point is that these abstractions *are* "believed"; they are the basis of political religions, though the political implications may seem contradictory. The energy of empire is equated with the energy of race, of the species, and that, of course, is reactionary in trend. At the same time, the energy of life in the species is also translatable into the political energy of the people, a revolutionary concept.[21] The final enemy of the Railroad Trust, the only power capable of breaking its grip, had to be the People. Here was a power that transcended individuals and came from nature; it had the strength of the species, a conquering strength condensed in the theme "the individual suffers, but the race goes on" (*O* 448). The People aroused are an "awakened brute," an "enraged beast"; but when the People are also a "god," as in Presley's vision, it is clear that the animal metaphors are there to endorse the life-force in collective humanity.[22]

To imagine the power of the Railroad and its money is to understand the stimulus for inventing the symbol of the People. On one side was corporate power—not human, but a machine alternately showing its face of steel or its face of paper, made of legal writ and money. On the other side, there is a gathering of victims but a possible reversal of their weakness to strength—to power with a human face. Again the political implications are strong. How do two collective abstractions negotiate with each other? They can't without contradicting their nature, their defined essence. Therefore, they fight in order that one, not the other, may survive. Violence is the necessary outcome of political allegory, one might say, since any other resolution—except, of course, the total enervation or decadence of one side—is inconsistent with the abstraction of historic conflict and rival powers.

In the background of this violence, this war of symbolic concepts, one sees an inherent moral irresponsibility in the "forces." But, as Shelgrim, the great corporate leader, suggests, the shift of responsibility to a "force" grants all the more license for violence in individuals. And we see in *The Octopus* that the very stress on group force tends to throw up a leader figure of giant proportions, for he is the symbol of that force. Shelgrim remains a threatening and omnipotent shadow, but Magnus Derrick, the leader of the ranchers, lives up to the proportions of his name until his final collapse. He has great personal magnetism—the force of his cause, his group identity, flows into him—and the ranchers can plausibly surrender to his power because, in terms of the novel, that power becomes their own.

Actually, as soon as Shelgrim identifies himself as an "ungovernable force," he suggests the existence of a force opposing him. The People, in battle with the "iron-hearted master of steel and steam," are equally ungovernable when enraged. Norris makes this explicit in the mob scene where the ranchers confront the railroad men at the Hooven ranch. As the alternative to passive drift and hopelessness, the "enraged beast" authorizes an explosive resistance, in any form it may take. Norris writes of a "war to the death" almost as a reflexive comment. This is more than rhetoric, for naturalist conflict tends to reach this extremity. The law of survival directs that two naturalist forces in conflict cannot remain in stalemate, nor, as I have said, can they negotiate without compromising their identity as a "force."

Ungovernable or enraged, a terrible power "not to be resisted," the People are nevertheless a welcome force because they represent the transference of power to a vitalist principle that attracts belief. On the model of Henry Adams, one might rather pray to it than to the Dynamo. The important need—and Norris's response to it is almost formulaic in the naturalist tradition of writing—is to make power humanly accessible and still do it justice, still mark out a stoic respect for nature's truth.

6 Vitalism and Redemptive Violence

Vitalism versus Mechanism

Near the last page of *The Octopus,* Norris proposed his naturalist theme as the conclusion for all narrative events.

> Men were naught, death was naught, life was naught: FORCE only existed—FORCE that brought men into the world, FORCE that crowded them out of it to make way for the succeeding generation. [*O* 436]

However, the intellectual unity of the novel does not rest on this narrow, despairing principle but rather on the effort to conquer its implications, to wrest from "FORCE" its own way of redemption, its own ethos of instruction. What could defend "life" and "men" against the endless implications of "naught" in generations and events moved only by "FORCE"? This cosmic theme is implicit in most of the imaginative constructions of political and literary naturalism that we know. The paradigm is Marxist: history's process and the naturalist theory of conflict lead dialectically to a just human society. The realities of power and conflict are not evaded; they are made use of.

If the monotheme of power presents the moral consciousness with a dilemma, it also presents a choice, as Henry Adams made clear when he made the images of the Virgin and the Dynamo tower over his pages. In an exact parallel, Frank Norris opposed the Railroad (leviathan with a heart of steel) to the land and its Wheat. Whatever the faults of the wheat-growers in their pursuit of power and profit, they still earn our sympathy against the operators of the machine. Explicitly, the loved women, Hilma and Angéle, share symbolism with the wheat. Angéle is the transcendent sign, loved by Vanamee, the mystic prophet, in both her first and second incarnations and worshiped both as a force and as a woman. The first Angéle was destroyed in a violent rape, a rather too obvious metaphor in the conflict between Wheat and Railroad. But the identification of woman and wheat makes it clear that all forms of naturalist force are not the same and that the one closest to vitalist nature can be redemptive and can be equated with love.

Vitalist nature is pitted against mechanical process and abstract social power and, above all, against the cold power of money. Presley, the poet, finds that his right destiny is to write a primitivist epic. "Life, the primitive simple direct Life, passionate, tumultous" (O 29), is the same divinity that Vanamee found and loved in Angéle: "It was one of those legendary passions that sometimes occur, idyllic, untouched by civilization, spontaneous as the growth of trees, natural as dewfall, strong as the firm-seated mountains" (O 26).

Vitalism is then a compensatory creed, the worship of a power that is acceptable and credible. Adams knew finally that he could pray better to the Virgin, or even to Venus, than to the Dynamo, which was more impersonal and mysterious than the movement of planets or the physics of motion. Dreiser moved less clearly in the same direction in *Sister Carrie*. The problem of man, he philosophized, is that of losing touch with the beneficent and welcome forces that rule existence. "As a beast the forces of life aligned with him . . .; as a man he has not yet learned how to align himself with the forces." The consequences of failing to do so can lead to extinction, prefaced by a desperate cynicism, as Presley learns from Shelgrim, the corporate leader, the man of shadow and mystery who says, "Blame conditions, not men." And Presley meditates:

> Was no one, then, to blame . . .? Forces, conditions, laws of supply and demand—were these then the enemies, after all? Not enemies; there was no malevolence in Nature. Colossal indifference only, a vast trend toward appointed goals. Nature was, then, a gigantic engine, a vast Cyclopean power . . . a prodigious mechanism of wheels and cogs. [O 396]

How does one align with a "colossal indifference"? Norris struggles valiantly with alternatives, including the most nihilistic, but in the end he turns toward an evolutionary vitalism as a defense against the "force" that crowds men out of the world. This turning is symbolized first in the reincarnation of Angéle in her daughter (to prove "there is no such thing as death" [O 437]) and then, more universally, in the elevation of the species over the individual: "The individual suffers, but the race goes on" (O 448). The Wheat survives all the death dealt out in its service, including, in particular, the death of Behrman, the railroad manager, who, trapped in a ship's hold, drowns in wheat. After that poetic justice, the Wheat goes onward in its voyage to feed the starving millions of India, a point Norris stresses in the novel's final paragraph.

Norris also found a direct way to associate Wheat, as life-force, with sexual energy and Woman. All three male protagonists are brought to experience this redemptive vitalist triad: Presley, the poet-seer, in general terms, Annixter, the macho rancher, in specific sexuality, and Vanamee, the mystic, in transcendental experience. The most explicit scene belongs to Annixter. Sexually driven toward his servant, Hilma Tree, and mistreating her in the process, he eventually discovers that he loves her and wants to marry her. This discovery is literally a revelation that comes to him on a morning when he notices the young wheat budding from the bare earth. It is this "strength of nations," this "force of the world" (not the rule of custom or morality) that moves him to what Norris exuberantly calls "the radiant magnificence of an inviolable pledge" (*O* 253).

Vanamee's scene is explicit in a different way, since his power is occult, and he has been trying to call the spirit of his dead and violated lover, Angéle, back to life. He succeeds without supernatural intervention, for the resurrected Angéle turns out to be her living daughter. Thus the man of occult powers and the man of earthly interests meet in intercourse with the natural Woman, herself the spirit of the Wheat. This, then, "the eternal renascent germ of life," a natural source of power, is Vanamee's moral anchorage.

This symbology leads to a dualistic or Manichean concept of natural forces, some that are congenial to man and others that are not, and the dichotomy operates as a profound structural principle both in Norris's *Octopus* and in other naturalist works. It may be the strongest moral inclination of naturalist thought and the secret of its capacity to generate political passion. This moral dualism responds to vitalist affirmations, first to a distinction between "life" forces and purely mechanical or material forces, and second to a distinction between the power of nature and the power of society—in Norris represented by the Wheat and the corporate Railroad. But Norris was also honestly reflective in his effort to face the intellectual dilemma posed by the fact that nature must in the end be *one* force, one process, not two. A simple moral dualism is also modified by his nonsentimental acknowledgment that life is harsh at any level—that it is, after all, a "force" and not a benevolent spirit.

These manifestations of ambivalence at the heart of the naturalist tradition are most significantly reflected in the works of Hemingway and Faulkner; but Norris, at an earlier stage, reveals the coexistence of naïve pastoral, or romantic primitivism, with a cult of stoic endurance of suffering. One of the ways in which monothematic naturalism tries to achieve philosophic unity is to draw a sympathetic principle out of pain by making suffering a part of an ultimately benign process. For example, the rape and

death of the first Angéle clearly lead to redemptive insight for
Vanamee and to a reincarnation of "the eternal renascent germ of
life" in the second Angéle. Simple primitivism, as Norris expressed
it, required moving back to get "in touch with the essential things,
back again to the starting point of civilization, coarse, vital, real,
and sane" (O 91). But "starting point" obviously does not refer to a
paradisial, precivilized state but to the chance to renew the cycle of
growth, to prove natural immortality, and, in the process, to re-
shape society and civilization. Since Norris had strong political
interests, the link with the cult of revolution, and its belief in the
purgative value of violent crises, is implicit in his pages. In any case,
vitalism is a better word than primitivism for describing Norris's
thematic ideas, and it relates to a strong tradition in modern vitalism that stresses the value of sacrifice and ordeal.[1]

In all of this Norris reveals a characteristic drive toward moral
judgments based on naturalist premises, but he also reveals, as I
have noted, the dichotomy in naturalist thinking, which alternates
between invoking the impersonal determinist process in events and
calling down a traditional moral judgment on the human agents of
the inhuman process. Thus, after devoting many pages to the ug-
liest possible portrait of human behavior in the men who represent
the Railroad, Norris leads Presley to "Blame conditions, not men."
However, to divorce judgments in this way from human beings
does not lessen the intensity of the resentment or resistance
aroused by "conditions" and "forces." To abstract an enemy may
result in abstracting one's resistance or in the license to use force
against force. Shelgrim was indeed successful in persuading Presley
not to kill him by convincing him that there are no enemies: there is
"no malevolence in Nature . . . only a vast trend toward appointed
goals" (O 396). This neutralizes Presley temporarily, but at the
same time it invokes the *deus ex machina* of naturalist fate by which
Behrman is killed, destroyed by the Wheat, whose appointed goals
find him in the way. The cruelty of Behrman's fate is a natural
cruelty; the accident that drowns him in wheat, as it pours into the
ship's hold, is morally neutral. No one shares in the responsibility
for this death, but everyone—that is, "everyone" projected in the
consciousness of the reader—assents to it. And though assent is all
that a natural force may require, assent is nonetheless significant
and consequential, particularly as it relates to the moral and political implications of Norris's ambitious epic novel.

That Norris found in vitalism a moral frame for the powerful
"forces" at work in his novel is verified by his use of a third force,
the People, to work with the Wheat and against the Railroad. As the

social conflict intensifies, the People become a poetic concept, a religious identity like the Wheat/Woman. The People are a "god" linked to vitalist energy, but at the same time they are an explicit moral agent, since they suffer from the absence of Wheat—as in India—and from the oppression of the Railroad Trust. Vanamee tells his poetic friend Presley, "Your inspiration has come *from* the People. Then let it go straight *to* the People" (*O* 258). One can act in their name, believing in them and feeling their inspiration even when the Wheat and the Land, even when the Woman, become blurred in a poetic haze.

The moral ambivalence in naturalist thought is squarely met and resolved by treating the People as a force. Since they are clearly the victims of power, all the pathos of victimization, and moral resentment against it, can be summoned on their behalf. But, for all that, they are ignorant of their own strength, which is terrible once it is aroused. And, since they are the People, whatever power they discover in themselves must be a just power, expressing a collectivized need in all their acts. Thus, populist sentiments parallel but ethically transcend concepts of race and empire. In the exuberant passage in which Annixter becomes aware of his strong love for Hilma simultaneously with his vision of the growing Wheat, the author speaks of the vital principle in both "as the strength of nations" (*O* 253).

Wheat is also the inspiration of Magnus Derrick's most grandiose imperial dream, which is echoed by other characters, including even the would-be epic poet, Presley.

> He [Derrick] saw only the grand *coup*, the huge results, the East conquered, the march of empire rolling westward, finally arriving at its starting point, the vague, mysterious Orient. He saw his wheat, like the crest of an advancing billow, crossing the Pacific, bursting upon Asia, flooding the Orient in a golden torrent. It was the new era. [*O* 219]

Magnus Derrick of all men had most wanted power: "To control men had ever been his ambition; submission of any kind, his greatest horror" (*O* 127). In the end he loses, just as the Railroad loses symbolically, or prophetically, in Behrman's death. Such defeats prove only that power is the cyclical law of life, ruling beyond the human values of the moment; its good is the right of necessity.

Accordingly, what Norris gives us is, in all its manifestations, a vitalist politics, a true metapolitics; its symbols—the People, the Woman, the Wheat—all lead to "the eternal renascent germ of life." This force, like Adams's Virgin, gathers saints, philosophers, and poets about itself, all the transcendent values Norris can summon, ranging from Vanamee's spirituality to Presley's great unwritten poem. Meanwhile, the same force can be relied on to subdue the selfish power asserted by individuals and even the rival corrupting forces thrown up by history: the power of money and of corporate society.

Violence as Ritual and Apocalypse

In *The Octopus* a floridly sensational fight takes place, described as an "abrupt swoop of terror and impending death . . . come and gone with the swiftness of a thunderclap" (*O* 180). This is violence in Norris's grand style. It occurs when Delaney, a drunken cowboy, infatuated with Hilma and jealous, breaks into Annixter's party, riding his horse into the room:

> He came with the suddenness of an explosion . . . . In a second of time the dance was a bedlam. The musicians stopped with a discord, and the middle of the crowded floor bared itself instantly. It was like sand blown from off a rock; the throng of guests, carried by an impulse that was not to be resisted, bore back against . . . each other, falling down, scrambling to their feet again, stepping over one another, getting behind each other, diving under chairs, flattening themselves against the wall—a wild, clamouring pell-mell, blind, deaf, panic-stricken; a confused tangle of waving arms, torn muslin, crushed flowers, pale faces, tangled legs, that swept in all directions back from the centre of the floor leaving Annixter and Hilma, alone, deserted, their arms about each other, face to face with Delaney, mad with alcohol, bursting with remembered insult, bent on evil, reckless of results. [*O* 176]

The author's temperament indulges in this rhetorical overkill to express the semisacred quality of violent experience, of life-turning revelations supported by transcendent sexuality, both in Annixter's fighting prowess, which defeats Delaney, and in Hilma's response to it. The same thing is true in *McTeague,* where violence is again linked with sex and both are touched with the awe of natural mystery. After a fumbling courtship, Trina is finally aroused by direct force:

> He had only to take her in his arms, to crush down her struggle with his enormous strength, to subdue her, conquer her by sheer brute force, and she gave up in an instant. [*Mc* 65]

Trina is no longer a specific woman, nor is McTeague the shambling inarticulate dentist we have known; a "force" has commanded

an instinct in awakening this woman: "Mysterious instincts as ungovernable as the winds of heaven were at work knitting their lives
together" (*Mc* 66). Later, when McTeague kills Trina in another
kind of brute embrace, the effect is to link sex and death in another
metaphysical unity, as if violence were the sign of all primary experiences and their common ground.

The role of violence is similarly mysterious in the story of Angéle
in *The Octopus*. She, of course, is the allegorical victim; and what
happens to her—a violent rape that leads to her death in child-
birth—is presented in a kind of abstract pantomime. The man-
beast who comes out of the night and disappears is identified only
as "that certain uncongeniality which . . . forever remains between
humanity and the earth which supports it" (*O* 124). But this interpretation of violence is complicated by the fact that Angéle herself
has been represented as a symbol of the life-force, a "Woman" *of*
the earth, and interpretation is further complicated by the strange
conclusion, when Angéle's daughter, the offspring of the sexual
violence, comes to her mother's inconsolable lover, Vanamee, bearing her mother's name and identity, to be loved again. The inter-
penetration of symbols was more than Norris could handle, but the
interesting result of it is the suggestion that the life-force appears to
be capable of revolting against itself. But perhaps all that is meant is
that violence is a metaphysical first principle in that it can—indeed,
must—be accepted as part of the ongoing life process.

The naturalist obsession with violence can, when conditioned by
an imaginative sensibility and raised to the level of revelation—
emerge in the form of ritual observations and ceremonial drama.
Stephen Crane had that kind of sensibility, tightening what is loose
allegory in Norris, and in *The Red Badge of Courage* he developed a
poetry of violence that singles that book out in the mainstream of
naturalist fiction.

Crane did not need to know the Civil War personally because he
knew it so well imaginatively; all that he needed were the naturalist
myths that fed his imagination. His book is powerful, standing out
above the works of Norris, London, and even Dreiser, not because
it documents the life of camp and battle but because it is highly
focused on primitive mysteries in battle and death.

Crane is clearly attempting to give a religious coloring to these
revelations. Nature contains a god, and his service is sacrifice and
death. War is nature's stormy Mount Sinai, "war, the red
animal—war, the blood-swollen god" (*RB* 23). All that nature contains of great force, pain, death, extreme physical effort, and ultimate physical collapse are given their high ground of revelation in
war. It is there that these naturalist truths meet and converge on a

metaphysical level. And when Henry Fleming is most absorbed by the battle, he knows war in this way: "He himself felt the daring spirit of a savage, religion—mad. He was capable of profound sacrifices, a tremendous death" (*RB* 103).

But since Henry is entirely oblivious of the political or moral justifications of this war, his battle crisis reveals only the cosmic processes of survival and death. Here can be found naturalism's nearest approach to religious transcendence, and it occurs at the boundaries of biological fate. And this is the essence of naturalist heroism: to approach the mystery of nature depends on the will to confront its most savage truth, sacrificing a mundane safety. Crane mentions "profound sacrifices," but it is clear that these sacrifices have no specific moral purpose. The value is metaphysical and personal, and the antagonist is not a human being but natural violence and death.

Violence possesses awesome meaning here because it opens toward death. The major confrontation with naturalist mystery is not in battle itself, for it comes to Henry Fleming when he is running away from battle. The scene is described in explicitly religious terms:

> he reached a place where the high, arching boughs made a chapel. He softly pushed the green doors aside and entered. Pine needles were a gentle brown carpet. There was a religious half light.
> Near the threshold he stopped, horror-stricken at the sight of a thing. [*RB* 41]

The "thing" is a dead man, seated with his back against a tree, and the chapel containing that thing expresses the lucid power of Crane's imagination. Crane of course complicates the religious references with the irony that is characteristic of all his writing, but here the irony is complex, not obviously reductive. Nothing of the shock of physical death is withheld; the eyes of the dead man have "the dull hue to be seen on the side of a dead fish," and

> Over the gray skin of the face ran little ants. One was trundling some sort of bundle along the upper lip. [*RB* 41]

In the midst of all this horror, "The dead man and the living man exchanged a long look." Then the scene draws softly to a close, as if it had brought spiritual comfort:

> The trees about the portals of the chapel moved soughingly in a soft wind. A sad silence was upon the little guarding edifice. [*RB* 42]

A fuller initiation into the mystery of death takes place later, in the prolonged agony of Henry's friend, Jim Conklin. As he walks beside Henry in the parade of the wounded, Jim is dying on his feet, staring into the unknown: "he seemed always looking for a place, like one who goes to choose a grave" (*RB* 47), and, already spectral in his look, he says, "don't tech me—leave me be" (*RB* 49). The dying man is preparing himself: "there was something ritelike in these movements of the doomed soldier" (*RB* 49). When the place and the moment are finally reached, there is an effect of ennoblement and transfiguration: "He was at the rendez-vous . . . there was a curious and profound dignity in the firm lines of his awful face" (*RB* 49, 50).

The dignity might reflect natural process: Conklin's last moment is like the falling of a tree, "a slight rending sound." But, with his mouth open, "the teeth showed in a laugh" (*RB* 50). The laugh dismisses a sentimental primitivism, and Conklin, when he falls, reveals the side of his body, which looks "as if it had been chewed by wolves." Fleming at this moment shakes his fist at the battlefield, getting out only one word, "Hell——." Following this is a line that has stirred debate among various critics as to its serious or ironic implication: "The red sun was pasted in the sky like a wafer."[2] Given the context, it would seem absurd to miss the irony of this reference to Christlike dying and to the Communion. Still, if Crane is here employing his characteristic irony, he is at the same time confirming the universal ritual modes for confronting the experience of death.

The allusion to Christ emphasizes the vulnerability of the religious imagination, a pathos that is frequent in naturalist writing. Here irony and pathos come together in the seeming laugh of the dying man, enforcing his stoic dignity. He dies as a tree falls, and he has chosen his place to die after walking for a long time with a horrible wound in his side. There is not only a natural mystery here but a moral lesson. Conklin himself has no doubt transcended the motivation of pride in his personal bearing, but Fleming seems to have learned something from it, and this is related to the ostensible theme of Crane's book, the "red badge" of an initiation into courage. Just as the mystery religions of nature reached their deepest revelations in death, so here a specifically naturalist ethic is death-oriented. Almost immediately after Conklin's death, which might have confirmed him more than ever in his desire to run away, Henry begins to envision, instead, a return to his comrades, among whom, restored to self-respect by leading a charge in battle, he sees himself "getting calmly killed before the eyes of all . . . . He thought of the magnificent pathos of his dead body" (*RB* 55).

The awe and fierce dignity of Conklin's death confirmed that "magnificent pathos." It is a death-pathos now linked to the spirit of "a savage religion" requiring "profound sacrifices." The forest chapel of death, where ants trailed over the dead soldier's lips, affirmed the harsh terms of a soldier's religion, and further, and conclusive, emphasis is placed on Henry's redemptive initiation in battle: "He had been to touch the great death, and found that, after all, it was but the great death. He was a man" (*RB* 109). The values of this manhood are vitalist, and Crane views their implications with detachment: "He had been where there was red of blood and black of passion, and he was escaped . . . . He saw that he was good" (*RB* 107). Did the "good" reside in Henry's escape or in his authentication by blood and passion? At that margin of experience it is not possible to distinguish between survival and authenticity, or self-realization.

Critics have argued about this conclusion of Crane's story. Some have accepted Fleming's apotheosis in courage, while others continue to challenge the notion that Crane was seriously attempting to define a code of virile honor. I doubt, myself, that Crane was capable of writing a line describing subjective human commitments without leaving the door open for implicit irony. He was that kind of naturalist—indeed, in his uncorrupted detachment he resembles Flaubert or Joyce—and it is from that perspective, with a lucidity that is almost inevitably ironic, that he viewed the male-oriented vitalism of hunting, fighting, and survival. In this he presents a precise contrast with Adams's cult of the Virgin. Yet it might seem that, moved by the same intellectual needs as Adams, Crane was led to a parallel sexual vitalism but one almost inevitably "machoist" in tendency (later to be elaborated in the works of Hemingway and Norman Mailer).

The naturalist ethic in which the red of blood and the black of passion are the banner of manhood and lead the way to the "good" finds easy reinforcement in the group. The battle ordeal and the natural laws of pain and death set the conditions for the "subtle battle brotherhood" of the men who fight together. In the end, after both loss and victory, the regiment has become "a mysterious fraternity born of the smoke and danger of death" (*RB* 31). The brotherhood of soldiers expresses the force of the vitalist cult as it might be applied to nations, races, and classes. These are collectivities committed to historic conflict and survival. Promoting the ethic of conflict, they learn to translate danger into fraternity; perhaps they even invite violence in order to learn fraternity.[3]

In Crane's completely clear view of this theme, the only suffering that exceeds physical suffering, and could make the latter welcome, is that of the moral outcast. Similarly, the only emotion that can compete with fear is shame. After Henry Fleming has run from battle, his fear lessens and he is gradually possessed by the self-ostracism of the moral refugee. As he walks among the wounded, he encounters the "tattered man," and the latter's desire to compare wounds probes into his cowardice. "The simple questions of the tattered man had been knife thrusts to him. They asserted a society" (*RB* 53). What Henry needs now is a wound of his own, and he longs for it, his "red badge of courage." The blow he receives from another fleeing soldier gives him what he wants, and he is able to return to his regiment. The wound is unworthy, but the link between its sign and his self-respect has been emphasized. Now he has the chance to redeem himself in another battle, and he does.

The power of emulation thus matches the power of pain and death. It is perhaps this equation in naturalist thought that is the key to some of its deepest political implications. Nature's force and process are absorbed and dominated by the social process, but this in turn is ruled by natural law. In an army the reasons for valuing courage and the ability to endure pain and face death are obvious. Nevertheless, Crane's descriptions of the army as a social unit and a moral force establish it as something much greater than an instrument for winning wars. His imagery is, as usual, concise and telling: "It [the regiment] inclosed him. And there were iron laws of tradition and law on four sides. He was in a moving box" (*RB* 21). The army as a thing, a box, alternates with images of the army as a serpent, a dragon, a monster. The interesting question is how this imagery supports rather than undercuts the army's function as a disciplined moral instrument, capable of collective judgment: "The regiment was like a firework" (*RB* 31), Crane writes, a thing ready to explode with its force. The point is actually to eliminate a traditional concept of judgment. This collectivity, enforcing behavior, is viewed as power in itself in its ability to evoke emulation, fear, shame, and pride.

The "naturalness" of this power is emphasized by the clarity with which Crane saw that to bring up the cause for fighting would have no relevance. There is no war here in the ordinary political and geographic sense. There are two armies, but they are distinguished only by the color of their uniforms. And the generals, who think they have control over the battle, actually do not. They send only inconsistent and incomprehensible orders, and they preside over actual confusion; for, whether running away or running forward, "the running men . . . were all deaf and blind" (*RB* 28).

Accordingly, when the group power of the army is not a prison-like enclosure of tradition and law, it becomes simply a "floodlike force." Either way, the species dominates, absorbs, and transcends individual instincts and all personal interests, including survival itself. The group is not led but driven, both from within and from

without; it either compulsively obeys tradition or anarchically surrenders to chaos. The army as a mob is as definite a force as the
army under discipline. Nothing really distinguishes this society
from simple organic or mechanical force except the spirit of
emulation. If the approach of battle reveals to Henry that "he knew
nothing of himself" and that "he was an unknown quantity" (*RB*
11), it also reveals that there is not much to know beyond the
realities of fear and courage, strength and weakness. For the rest,
"he continually tried to measure himself by his comrades" (*RB* 14);
it was their good opinion he wanted. Henry's mind is at times filled
with conventional battle romanticism, with notions of breathless
deeds observed by "heavy crowns and high castles," but this traditional idealization of war is treated as a thin layer of childlike fantasy superimposed on more basic forces: the "moving box" of the
army and the "throat-grappling" instinct for battle.

Still, as I have noted, these more basic forces are themselves the
source of idealizations, of purely naturalist values. One is the vitalist virtue of proven manhood, of macho courage. Another is
Henry's feeling of sublimity in the presence of "tremendous death"
or in "the magnificent pathos of his [own] dead body" (*RB* 55). This
might be called the moral code of Thanatos, calling for "an enthusiasm of unselfishness," "a sublime recklessness . . . shattered
against the iron gates of the impossible" (*RB* 103). The highest
virtue learned in naturalist conflict thus seems to be self-
immolation. Behind war, "the blood-swollen god," stands death, a
greater god, and the question that needs review is the extent to
which the naturalist myth finds itself in service to the gods of
greatest strength. The death pathos has no rival in its power to stir
human emotions; recognizing this, Crane went further than most
naturalist writers in appreciating the primitive compulsions of attraction and dread that death exerts.

Let us then trace the clear outline of Crane's naturalist values.
Primordial violence, "the red animal," releases the most elemental
and unsocialized passions and instincts. But since in Crane's work
this occurs in the context of opposed armies, it results in elemental
socialization. Henry Fleming's only defense against the fear of
death, and perhaps against the attractions of death, is the approval
of his comrades. He knew his greatest despair when he was alone,
isolated from the rest of the army. Confronting death, he comes
back to the army and experiences great relief, as if here was the
only alternative to metaphysical panic. Social membership is almost
as absolute as death, and it receives from death a kind of existential
sanction, giving to Henry all the confidence of being that he can
have. In all of this the crisis of violence is indispensable, for it

proves the need for high group discipline and, in a naturalist paradox, juxtaposes primitive savagery with highly organized behavior. The battle scene brings together the reality of power and conflict and a primitive social ethic at its point of inception. In fact, if one wonders why the ethos of naturalist political movements, whether fascist or communist, is imbued with authoritarian discipline, the most direct answer would be that, in assuming the universality of group conflict as the premise for their existence, they needed to organize and motivate themselves like armies.

Redemptive Violence

In *The Red Badge of Courage*, a novel of war, where the opportunity to expose social illusions and oppressions was most available, Crane chose to concentrate on primitive collective psychology and instinctual experience. He pointedly avoids the social and historical issues of the Civil War. The deepest reading of Crane, I myself believe, emphasizes a tragic naturalism or a pessimism directed at both natural violence and social rule. But it is arguable, to a degree limited somewhat by his ironic sensibility, that Crane, in both *Maggie* and *The Red Badge of Courage*, is a vitalist in whom high respect for truth fuses with stoic faith in nature. Certainly he traces the growth of a neoprimitive, stoic religion of nature in his characters, as in Henry Fleming's inchoate respect for the gods of death and war. Essential to it is the ordeal, the arena in which the hero finds value in pain, violence, and even death—accepts them as productive of good. The ethos that naturalism develops is thus based on the struggle for survival, and it features that combination of sacrificial and stoic virtues described by Lovejoy as "hard primitivism."[4] Nietzsche was the modern teacher of these stoic values when he said, in making his own great claim to naturalist revelations, that he would rather perish than renounce the truth that "life sacrifices itself—for the sake of power!"[5] The various forms of redemptive or cathartic violence expressed in the works of Crane and Hemingway and by many later disciples, in both fiction and film, are specifically Nietzschean motifs in the modern myth of power.[6]

As Nietzsche's own language declares, the virtues of power require sacrifice, even a heightened capacity for suffering. I have noted how Crane, Norris, and Dos Passos (in *USA*) all illustrate a significant anomaly in naturalist fiction; namely, they see violence as the motive force of all action, yet they attack the moral hypocrisy of societies and their repression and abuse of human beings. Nature is rough and merciless, but society mendaciously cripples humanity with antinatural codes of behavior and so bars the road to the full life. This double perspective is the key to understanding some of the most meaningful general patterns of naturalist writing. The cruelty of nature may be magnified in order to assail idealizing fictions, and a drama develops in which violence, pain, and shock are offered as purifying experiences. But it may also follow that pain and shock are the gateways to genuine naturalist fulfillment: the door of truth opens for the hero after much testing of his endurance, and, at the end, his reward is not only authenticity but the fully expressed life.

In brief, a form of naturalist redemption is available, one that requires not only the destruction of lies and repressive taboos but also the ability to endure cruelty and meet violence on its own terms. The cult of risking death and pain is part of an effort to live according to nature. When Nietzsche said that life sacrifices itself for the sake of power, he clearly meant that life is most to be celebrated in its climaxes of destruction, as in the "perishing and falling of leaves." This apocalyptic God-in-nature best reveals himself in extreme ordeals, at life's margins. True revelation, for both the individual and communities, is accompanied by a drama of violence and overturning.

Frank Norris, in his usual direct way, pointed to this in his fiction when he called for "vast and terrible dramas," for "blood and sudden death,"[7] and Stephen Crane brought his soldier onto the battlefield to experience that sort of terrible drama. The origin of these dramatic intensities is almost surely in Zola's original concept of radical experimentation (in the dissecting room, he said) as the basis of naturalist fiction. But writers like Norris and Jack London carried the apocalypse beyond experiment or ritual to the point where violence is no longer a metaphor but the essence of life, the culmination of human experience. In *The Call of the Wild*, the hunting kill is the model for life at its climax, and authenticated, endowed life is awarded to the victor at the expense of the loser:

> There is an ecstasy that marks the summit of life, and beyond which life cannot rise . . .; this ecstasy comes when one is most alive . . . comes to the artist, caught up and out of himself in a sheet of flame; it comes to the soldier, war-mad on a stricken field and refusing quarter; and it came to Buck, leading the pack, sounding the old wolf-cry, straining after the food that was alive . . . . He was mastered by the sheer surging of life, the tidal wave of being, the perfect joy of each separate muscle, joint, and sinew in that it was everything that was not death, that it was aglow and rampant, expressing itself in movement, flying exultantly under the stars and over the face of dead matter that did not move.[8]

The revulsion from "dead matter" is the significant basis of this ecstasy, and it exhibits the typical trend of naturalist fiction toward apocalyptic climaxes. It also suggests a need for transcendence, even under naturalist limitations—not transcendence beyond natural experience but *within* it, through intensifications of it, either as esthetic re-creations or in sensory ecstasy. This may be the only way to adapt value judgments to power theory. If power is the law of life, then the striving of human characters becomes an effort to *share* power, to experience it not as victim but as agent. The movement of individual existence then becomes one of force answering force, extracting a violence identified with life or identifying instinctual strength as the one force available to the human will, to be called one's own.

In Richard Wright's *Native Son* this struggle is expressed in two symbolically intensified murders. No reader forgets the excess of violence in Bigger Thomas's murder of Mary, the wealthy white girl, when, after strangling her, he must slice off her head before he can force her body into a furnace. That murder was partly accidental, but, during it and afterward, Bigger's motive for killing is aroused on a level deeper than self-preservation or his conflict with white society. Max, Bigger's lawyer and a politically sympathetic Communist, makes an eloquent defense by citing the social hatred that had led to the murder. But even Max is finally shocked and frightened by Bigger's revelation that in killing Mary he was exhilarated by a new sense of his own strength and freedom: "The feeling of being always enclosed in the stifling embrace of an invisible force had gone from him." And in his last words to Max, Bigger says something more:

> "I didn't want to kill!" Bigger shouted. "But what I killed for, I am. It must've been pretty deep in me to make me kill! I must have felt it awful hard to murder.... What I killed for must've been good!" Bigger's voice was full of frenzied anguish. "It must have been good! When a man kills, it's for something.... I didn't know I was really alive in this world until I felt things hard enough to kill for 'em.... It's the truth, Mr. Max."[9]

The interesting political note here is Bigger's strangely abstract assumption that an act of violence can be *for* something—that, if it is sufficiently compelled, felt deeply enough, it is required by some ultimately beneficial process and so becomes a "good." But beyond the abstract general struggle, dictated, no doubt, by the ideological convictions of the author, Bigger expresses his personal need for a redemptive act of self-assertion. His personal and political fates have been footnoted and explained by naturalist fate, with violence having, in effect, the sacerdotal function of authenticating these three dimensions of his existence. By contrast, the act of society in executing Bigger is abstract and cold, enveloped in the rationalizations of racial prejudice and political fear. For a sympathetic reader, weighing the justice of these acts of killing, Bigger's celebration of being "alive in this world" may be morally convincing.[10] Pragmatic justifications of violence have been left behind. The murders Bigger commits are almost a blessed infliction: at their minimum value, they guarantee the state of truth; at their maximum, they promise social and personal salvation.

In summary, then, apocalyptic themes in naturalist writing reflect the traditional need for metaphysical judgment. There will always be analogies for the story of Cain, the Flood, Sodom, and the Crucifixion. But now that the mystery of nature has retired within itself, it has become immanent in man. Revelation becomes a drastic necessity on this earthly ground of authentic suffering. In some imaginative extremes of naturalist writing, to force a life to its crisis becomes a matter of honor; one must seek the climaxes of pain, just as one seeks the climaxes of pleasure. A metaphysical imperative replaces what was only a temptation to purely instinctual or primitive experience. And whether naturalist revelation prophesies the ultimate apocalypse or teaches nothing but stoic endurance of animal fate, one can be certain from the evidence of the literature that a whole structure of dependent values may be built on the harsh lessons of violence.

Notes

Preface

1. Wallace Stevens, "The Noble Rider and the Sound of Words," *The Necessary Angel* (New York: Knopf, 1951).

Chapter One

1. Anthony Burgess, *New York Times Book Review*, 25 September 1977, p. 45.
2. Bertrand Russell, *Power* (New York: Norton, 1938), p. 12.
3. George Santayana, "The Elements and Function of Poetry," *Interpretations of Poetry and Religion* (New York: Harper, 1957), p. 284.
4. Julien Benda, *The Betrayal of the Intellectuals*, trans. Richard Aldington (Boston: Beacon Press, 1955), p. 99.
5. Ralph Waldo Emerson, *The Complete Works* (Cambridge, Mass.: Riverside Press, 1903), vol. 2, p. 60. (Subsequently referred to as *ECW*.)
6. Theodore Dreiser, *Newspaper Days* (New York: Liveright, 1922), pp. 457–59.
7. In Arthur O. Lovejoy and George Boas, eds., *A Documentary History of Primitivism and Related Ideas* (Baltimore: Johns Hopkins University Press, 1935), pp. 9–11.
8. *Beyond Good and Evil*, trans. Marianne Cowan (Chicago: Regnery, 1955), p. 160.
9. Ibid., p. 201.
10. *Thus Spake Zarathustra*, trans. R. S. Hollingdale (Baltimore: Penguin Books, 1962), p. 138.
11. Ibid., p. 136.
12. Stephen Crane, *The Red Badge of Courage* (New York: Norton, 1976), p. 103. (First published, 1895.) (Subsequently referred to as *RB*.)
13. See Henry Binder, "The Red Badge of Courage Nobody Knows," *Studies in the Novel* 10 (Spring 1978): 9–47.

Chapter Two

1. Emile Zola, *The Experimental Novel*, trans. Belle M. Sherman (New York: Haskell House, 1964), pp. 25–26.
2. *The Education of Henry Adams*, ed. Ernest Samuels (Boston: Houghton Mifflin, 1973), p. 36.
3. Herbert Spencer, *Social Statics* (New York: Appleton, 1910), p. 206. (First published in 1864.)
4. Luigi Pirandello, quoted by Alastair Hamilton, *The Appeal of Fascism* (New York: Macmillan, 1971), p. 45.
5. Ibid., p. 47.
6. Ibid.
7. Gottfried Benn, quoted by Hamilton, ibid., p. 151.

8. *Hitler's Words*, ed. Gordon W. Prange (Washington, D.C.: American Council on Public Affairs, 1944), p. 8.

9. "[For] our aim in foreign policy . . . *to secure for the German people the land and soil to which they are entitled on this earth* . . . would make any sacrifice in blood seem justified; before God, since we have been put on this earth with the mission of eternal struggle for our daily bread, beings who receive nothing as a gift, and who owe their position as lords of the earth only to the genius and the courage with which they can conquer and defend it" (*Mein Kampf*, trans. Ralph Manheim [London: Hutchinson, 1969], p. 596).

10. Ibid., p. 60.

11. *Selected Correspondence, Marx and Engels, 1846–1895* (London: Lawrence & Wishart, 1936), p. 125.

12. Jacques Ellul, *Autopsy of Revolution*, trans. Patricia Wolf (New York: Knopf, 1971), p. 89.

13. D. H. Lawrence, *Apocalypse* (London: Martin Secker, 1932), p. 94.

14. Isaiah Berlin has led the way in examining this aspect of nineteenth-century thought; in a recent review article he speaks of the "vast, visionary utopias of socialists and Catholics, Hegelians and positivists and many another among the great metaphysical and religious system-builders of the nineteenth century." It was an age, as Berlin sums it up, of "vast cosmologies which minimize the role of the individual, curb his freedom, repress his desire to self-expression, and order him to humble himself before the great laws and institutions of the universe, immovable, omnipotent, and everlasting, in whose sight free human choice is but a pathetic illusion" (*New York Review of Books*, 19 April 1979, p. 19).

15. *The Centenary Edition of the Works of Thomas Carlyle*, ed. H. D. Traill (London: Chapman & Hall, 1896–99), vol. 5, pp. 56–57.

16. Philip Rosenberg, *The Seventh Hero* (Cambridge, Mass.: Harvard University Press, 1974).

17. Carlyle, *Works*, vol. 1, p. 156. Rosenberg points out that this maxim was intended for politics as well as religion, "for at a time when doubts have arisen as to what men's rights are, the only way of settling these doubts is to test them in the crucible of political struggle" (*The Seventh Hero*, p. 138).

18. Georg Wilhelm Friedrich Hegel, *The Philosophy of History*, trans. J. Sibree (New York: Dover, 1956), p. 10. Rosenberg observes that Carlyle refers very little to the works of Hegel, close as he was to German thinkers and writers and to the context in which Hegel wrote and enforced his own influence; see *The Seventh Hero*, p. 12.

19. Carlyle, *Works*, vol. 4, p. 2; Rosenberg, *The Seventh Hero*, p. 139.

20. Ellul, *Autopsy of Revolution*, p. 128.

21. Sir Isaiah Berlin, *Karl Marx* (London: Oxford University Press, 1963), p. 128:

[History's] essence is the struggle of men to realize their full human potentialities; and, since they are members of the natural kingdom (for there is nothing that transcends it), man's effort to realize himself fully is a striving to escape from being the plaything of forces that seem at once mysterious, arbitrary, and irresistible, that is, to attain to the mastery of them and of himself, which is freedom. Man attains this subjugation of his world not by increase in knowledge obtained by contemplation (as Aristotle had supposed) but by activity—by labour—the conscious moulding by men of their environment and of each other—the first and most essential form of the unity of will and thought and deed, of theory and practice.

22. Ibid., p. 64.

23. The ultimate debasement of neo-Hegelian doctrine, we suppose, came with Hitler's pathological self-confidence in his campaign of destruction. "The men I

want around me," he said, "are those who, like myself, see in force the motive element in history, and who act accordingly." Taking this nourishment from historic necessity, his gamble in going to war in 1939 was in his own mind not a gamble, as Joachim Fest has pointed out, since it was prompted by his deducing the "certainty of victory from the processes of history" (Fest, *The Face of the Third Reich* [New York: Pantheon, 1970], pp. 297, 50). Perhaps he saw also that his deadliest rivals for this historic justification were the Communists, who were far more articulate than he in charting history's course.

24. Karl Marx, *The Economic and Philosophical Manuscripts of 1844*, ed. Dirk J. Struik, trans. Martin Milligan (New York: International Publishers, 1964), p. 135.

25. Berlin, *Karl Marx*, p. 87.

26. The crossing of Darwinism with Adam Smith's doctrine was most directly expressed by Walter Bagehot, who was one of the first to make a conscious effort to translate scientific principles into politics. Laissez-faire economics was rooted in the natural-law tradition, but it too benefited from the notion of evolutionary progress. To quote Bagehot, "The energy of civilization grows by the coalescence of strengths and the competition of strengths" (*Physics and Politics* [New York: Knopf, 1948], p. 53 [first published in 1875]).

27. Sigmund Freud, *Civilization and Its Discontents*, trans. James Strachey (New York: Norton, 1962), p. 69. (First publication in English, 1930.)

28. To illustrate the far-ranging influence of Freud's ethos-bearing dialectic, one could refer here to a rather narrow if sensational contemporary theory of poetry. Harold Bloom proposes that every poem and the work of every poet expresses a struggle not only with father precursors but with anticipated sons and followers. Here is the way a reviewer of Bloom's *A Map of Misreading* (New York: Oxford University Press, 1975) summarized this theme, which had appeared also in Bloom's earlier work, *The Anxiety of Influence* (New York: Oxford University Press, 1973):

> No text can be complete because on the one hand it is an attempt to struggle free of earlier texts impinging on it, and, on the other, it is preparing itself to savage texts not yet written by authors not yet born . . . . Instead of texts and authors, there are wills struggling to overcome other wills, there are patricides and infanticides whose paradox is that poetry is, if not the manifest result of such violence, then the constantly impressive evidence. [Edward W. Said, *New York Times Book Review*, 13 April 1975]

It would be difficult to find a more trenchant example of naturalist struggle, even violence, seen as a creative, ultimately beneficial force.

29. Lawrence, *Apocalypse*, p. 66.

30. Ibid., pp. 160–62. Lawrence's most sincere disciple in contemporary writing is probably Norman Mailer, who in his essay "The White Negro," celebrating that sophisticated naturalist hero the "hipster," made this summary statement of a vitalist creed:

> to be with it is to have grace, is to be closer to the secrets of that inner unconscious life which will nourish you if you can hear it, for you are then nearer to that God which every hipster believes is located in the senses of his body, that trapped, mutilated and nonetheless megalomaniacal God who is It, who is energy, life, sex, force, the Yoga's *prana*, the Reichian's orgone, Lawrence's "blood," Hemingway's "good," the Shavian life-force; "It"; God; not the God of the churches but the unachievable whisper of mystery within the sex, the paradise of limitless energy and perception just beyond the next wave of the next orgasm. ["The White Negro," *Advertisements for Myself* (New York: Putnam, 1959), p. 351]

This god that Mailer worships is not exactly the god of Henry Adams, who worshiped Venus in the Virgin. She possessed the same vitalist essence, but modern vitalism is truly daimonic, not sentimental or primitivist; it comes to us under the authority of Lawrence and Nietzsche, and they, of course, made a deep difference. Second, Mailer's hipster god is presented under psychological auspices; Freud and Reich are there to define him (as well as that therapeutic terrorist, Frantz Fanon, as interpreted by Sartre), and his force, in large part, is from within, blessing strength but also perception. The ambivalence is modern and quite radical; the apocalypse of violence comes bearing gifts, if not that of a new civilization, then at least that of psychic health. The point is that there is a basis for being *blessed;* Mailer writes of "a paradise of limitless energy," and this indicates how far the myth of power has come since the time when Dreiser talked bleakly of life as a speck or atom of aimless energy.

31. Lawrence, *Apocalypse,* p. 163.

32. Berlin, *Karl Marx,* p. 55.

33. Ibid., pp. 126–27.

34. Pierre-Joseph Proudhon, *General Idea of the Revolution in the Nineteenth Century,* trans. John B. Robinson (London: Freedom Press, 1923), p. 40. (Originally published in French in 1852.)

35. Georges Sorel, *Reflections on Violence,* trans. T. E. Hulme and J. Roth (New York: Free Press, 1950), p. 150. (Originally published in French in 1906.)

36. Ibid., pp. 137, 135.

37. Ibid., p. 209.

38. Ibid., p. 167.

39. Reported in the *New York Times,* 7 February 1974, p. 3, from the original article appearing in the Party's theoretical journal, *Hung Chi,* in 1966.

40. Giuseppe Prezzolini in *La Rivoluzione Liberale,* 7 December 1922, quoted by Alastair Hamilton, *The Appeal of Fascism,* p. 48.

41. John R. Harrison, *The Reactionaries* (London: Gollancz, 1966), p. 169.

42. Hannah Arendt, *On Violence* (New York: Harcourt, Brace & World, 1970), p. 69.

43. Ibid., p. 75.

44. Antonin Artaud, "The Theater of Cruelty (First Manifesto)," *The Theater and Its Double,* trans. Mary C. Richards (New York: Grove Press, 1958), p. 99.

45. Thomas Mann, *Politische Schriften und Reden* (Frankfurt a/M, 1968), p. 10, quoted by Hamilton, *The Appeal of Fascism,* p. 96.

46. Benedetto Croce, *Materialismo storico ed economia marxistica,* 9th ed. (Bari, 1951), p. xiii; quoted and translated by H. Stuart Hughes, *Consciousness and Society* (New York: Random House/Vintage, 1961), p. 249.

47. Walter B. Rideout, *The Radical Novel in the United States* (Cambridge, Mass.: Harvard University Press, 1956), pp. 41, 54.

48. The words "human solidarity" come from Camus in exactly the right context. He, more than anyone, deeply desired to humanize and moralize the harsh rule of naturalist conflict. He therefore contemplated the civilizing mission of "the rebel":

> He is acting on behalf of a value that is as yet confused but which he senses is a common bond among all men . . . . Yet the foundation of this value is the revolt itself. Human solidarity is built upon the act of revolt, and the latter in turn finds its sole justification in this complicity. [Quoted by Ellul, *Autopsy of Revolution,* p. 22]

Reversing the issue, a recent widely discussed book on the Holocaust attempted to endow the victims of violence, not "rebels," with the reward of discovered human solidarity, for the evidence of thousands of acts of comfort and help among the victims proved that the most radical violence did not destroy community but restored it and gave it the deepest moral significance (see Terrence Des Pres, *The Survivor* [New York: Oxford University Press, 1976]).

49. C. Wright Mills, *The Power Elite* (New York: Oxford University Press, 1959), p. 3.

50. Ibid. Hitler recognized how alluring power could be to the powerless, and this knowledge was a great asset in his naturalistic politics, as noted by Fest: "He made it possible for [his followers] to overcome the consciousness of their own weakness by equating themselves with a supposedly elemental force" (*The Face of the Third Reich*, pp. 297–98).

51. Lionel Trilling, *Beyond Culture* New York: Viking Press, 1965), pp. xii–xiii.

52. Jean-Jacques Lebel, "Theory and Practice," *New Writers IV: Plays and Happenings* (London: Calder & Boyars, 1967), pp. 33, 24, 21. A more impressive authority endorsed the view that war and art are linked both literally and metaphorically: Thomas Mann, who indulged his taste for a military combination of violence and order in the World War I period:

> That victorious, warlike principle of today, organization, is the basic principle, the essence of Art. . . . Endurance, precision, circumspection, boldness, courage in the face of hardship and defeat in the battle with solid matter; contempt for what is known as "security" in bourgeois life . . . the habit of a dangerous, tense, attentive existence . . . all these things are both military and artistic. [*Politische Schriften und Reden* (Frankfurt a/M, 1968), vol. 2, p. 8; quoted by Hamilton, *The Appeal of Fascism*, p. 96]

It is evident that artists are surrogate aristocrats, as Ezra Pound would be saying during the same years. But, even before that, the line between politics and art had been erased by Marinetti and the Futurists. The latter declared their lust for war in these words: "It is only with violence that we can restore the idea of justice . . . only then can we restore heroism" (F. T. Marinetti, *Democrazia futurista, dinamismo politico* [Milan, 1919], p. 224; quoted by Hamilton, p. 20). Here violence and art, order and war, are not conjunctions of desperate last resort; they are supreme values, serving justice and reviving heroism. The language suggests the redemptive metapolitics of Sorel, who indeed must have been a chief influence for avant-garde neopolitical ideology.

53. André Breton, *Manifestoes of Surrealism*, trans. Richard Seaver and Helen R. Lane (Ann Arbor: University of Michigan Press, 1969), p. 125.

54. Artaud, *The Theater and Its Double*, pp. 102, 114.

55. Ibid., p. 122.

56. Breton, *Manifestoes of Surrealism*, p. 125.

57. Ibid., p. 123.

58. Jean-Paul Sartre, *What Is Literature*, trans. Bernard Frechtman (New York: Harper, 1956), p. 214.

59. Paul Tillich, *The Protestant Era* (Chicago: University of Chicago Press, 1957), p. 196.

60. Norman Mailer has provided some accurate present-day evocations of the spirit of the old avant-garde, with the artist playing the role of warrior hero, confronting the margins of experience, and reaping the neoreligious and artistic rewards. The artist, he says, must be one of those who have "the courage to pay the hard price of full consciousness" (*Advertisements for Myself*, p. 23).

> The good artist [tries] to discover what it is all about. Realism was a way of moving into this modern mystery. But there has been so much work done that violence appeals to the artist now because it is the least tangible, the least explored frontier . . .; to write about violence is always an act of creation. [Interview published in *Twentieth Century* 173 (1964–65): 109–14; reprinted in *Violence in the Streets*, ed. Shalom Endelman (Chicago: Quadrangle, 1968), pp. 89–90]

61. Hamilton quotes Ernst Jünger:

Modern Nationalism . . . wants the extraordinary. . . . It does not want moderation. . . . The father of Nationalism is war. . . . War is the experience of blood, so all that matters is what *men* have to say about it. . . . Thus our values should be heroic values, the values of warriors and not of shopkeepers. . . . We do not want what is useful, practical and agreeable, but that which is necessary and desired by fate. [Hamilton, *The Appeal of Fascism,* pp. 121–22]

62. Filippo T. Marinetti, *Selected Writings,* trans. Arthur A. Coppotelli and R. W. Flint (New York: Farrar, Straus & Giroux, 1971), p. 41.

63. Stephen Spender, review of John Willett's *Art and Politics in the Weimar Period* (New York: Pantheon, 1979) in *The New York Review of Books* 26 (5 April 1979): 23. Anyone now writing on this theme must acknowledge a debt to Frank Kermode, particularly for the chapter "The Modern Apocalypse" in his *The Sense of an Ending* (New York: Oxford University Press, 1967). Discussing Yeats, Pound, Lewis, and Eliot as the modernist masters, Kermode sees them as first examples of "that correlation between early modernist literature and authoritarian politics which is more often noticed than explained: totalitarian theories of form matched or reflected by totalitarian politics" (p. 108). It is my hope here to advance that project of explanation.

64. Artaud, *The Theater and Its Double,* pp. 31–32.

65. Ibid., p. 13. Note, particularly, Artaud's dichotomy of "forms" and "force": "If our life lacks brimstone, i.e., a constant magic, it is because we choose to observe our acts and lose ourselves in considerations of their imagined form instead of being compelled by their force" (p. 8).

66. Ibid., p. 13.

67. Françoise Gilot and Carlton Lake, *Life with Picasso* (New York: McGraw-Hill, 1964), p. 59.

68. Ibid., p. 272.

69. Wallace Stevens, *The Necessary Angel,* p. 22.

70. Ibid., p. 36.

Chapter Three

1. George Santayana, *Interpretations of Poetry and Religion* (New York: Scribner's, 1900), p. 223.

2. All of the quotations from Emerson are from "The Poet" (*ECW* 3:17, 20, 15, 42).

3. Herman Melville, *Moby-Dick,* ed. Harrison Hayford and Hershel Parker (New York: Norton, 1967), pp. 169, 416, 144, 148.

4. Cited by Zoltan Haraszti, *John Adams and the Prophets of Progress* (Cambridge, Mass.: Harvard University Press, 1952), p. 219.

5. *The Education of Henry Adams,* edited by Ernest Samuels (Boston: Houghton Mifflin, 1973), p. 474. (Subsequently referred to as *E.*)

6. There is no resisting the surmise that Adams would have sided with Ezra Pound in his "esthetic politics" and that he would have joined postnaturalist intellectuals like Marinetti and D'Annunzio in welcoming Mussolini. As M. L. Rosenthal has noted, Pound defended Mussolini's methods as "not unscrupulous but creative; 'the opportunism of the artist'" (*The Modern Poets* [New York: Oxford University Press, 1965], p. 61). Pound himself declared his aristocratic and esthetic politics this way:

The artist has been at peace with his oppressors for long enough. He had dabbled in democracy and he is not done with that folly . . . . The aristocracy of entail and title has decayed, the aristocracy of commerce is decaying, the aristocracy of the arts is ready again for its service . . .; we artists who have been so long despised are about to take over control. ["The New Sculpture," *The Egoist,* 16 February 1914, p. 68]

7. Henry Adams, *Mont-Saint-Michel and Chartres* (New York: Doubleday, 1959), p. 301. (Privately printed in 1904; first published in 1913.) (Subsequently referred to as *MSM.*)

8. Leo Marx, *The Machine in the Garden* (New York: Oxford University Press, 1964), p. 350.

9. Michael Colacurcio, "The Dynamo and the Angelic Doctor: The Bias of Henry Adams' Medievalism," *American Quarterly* 17 (Winter 1965): 711.

10. Robert E. Spiller, essay on Adams in *Literary History of the United States,* ed. Robert E. Spiller, Willard Thorp, et al., 4th rev. ed. (New York: Macmillan, 1974), p. 1102.

11. Robert Mane, *Henry Adams on the Road to Chartres* (Cambridge, Mass.: Harvard University Press, 1971), pp. 194–244. Mane's work is valuable both for its intensive study of Adams's maneuvering between fact and fantasy and for its discerning judgment of the work of other critics.

12. Ibid., p. 225.

13. Ernest Samuels indicates that Adams quickly responded to Bergson's ideas in 1909, the year *Creative Evolution* was first published. He also points out that Adams, though he approved of this revival of vitalism, wished to use Bergson's ideas as an instrument with which to attack Darwinian optimism. This caused him to oppose Bergsonian affirmations, "ingeniously twisting," as Samuels says, "the vitalist critique of mechanistic evolution in order to show the way to an even more formidable determinism than the mechanists propounded" (*Henry Adams: The Major Phase* [Cambridge, Mass.: Harvard University Press, 1964], p. 466). Samuels is right in seeing the more uncompromising naturalist basis of Adams's form of vitalism. A letter Adams wrote to Albert S. Cook in 1910 describes his adaptation of Bergsonian ideas, particularly in relation to his *Mont-Saint-Michel and Chartres:*

> I wanted to show the intensity of the vital energy of a given time, and of course that intensity had to be stated in its two highest terms—religion and art . . . . My idea is that the world outside—the so-called modern world—can only pervert and degrade the conceptions of the primitive instinct of art and feeling, and that our only chance is to accent the limited number of survivors—the one-in-a-thousand of born artists and poets—and to intensify the energy of feeling within that radiant centre. In other words, I am a creature of our poor old Calvinistic St. Augustinian fathers, and am not afraid to carry out my logic to the vigorous end of regarding our present society, its ideals and purposes, as dregs and fragments of some primitive, essential instinct now nearly lost. If you are curious to see the theory stated as official instruction, you have only to look over Bergson's *Evolution Créatrice.* The tendencies of thought in Europe seem to me very strongly that way. [*The Letters of Henry Adams,* ed. Worthington C. Ford (Boston: Houghton Mifflin, 1938), vol. 2, pp. 546–47]

14. In reference to this anthropological interest in sex, Ernest Samuels points to a possible source in the preface to Havelock Ellis's *Studies in the Psychology of Sex:* "I regard sex as the central problem of life . . .; the question of sex—with the racial questions that rest on it—stands before the coming generations as the chief problem for solution" (quoted by Samuels, "Henry Adams' 20th Century Virgin," *Christian Century* 77 [1960]: 1143–60).

15. *Letters,* ed. Ford, vol. 2, p. 457. I believe that Mane, who also quotes this letter, blurs a point when he stresses Adams's detachment from sexual feeling and, in rebutting Ernest Samuels, says that "it is as much a mistake to examine this heroine

[the Virgin] in an anthropological or biological light as it is to assess her from the theological point of view" (*Henry Adams on the Road to Chartres*, p. 200). It is true that Adams gives us neither a convincing paganism nor an accurate theology. But why should that matter, since his purpose was to find the order, the moral energy, that Mary provided to a civilization? Adams was not a primitivist or vitalist in the sense of wishing to reduce his goddess to images of sexual or maternal experience. Being a highly sublimated man himself, he wanted to trace the sources of sublimated energy. Furthermore, there is no reason to question his regret for the lack of sexual vitality in his own culture; the lack of it in his writing (which seems to be what Mane is pointing out) is part of the evidence for that regret.

Chapter Four

1. The one whom Adams is really recalling here is, of course, Carlyle, for whom he had a much greater affinity.

2. Henry David Thoreau, *Walden*, ed. Sherman Paul (Boston: Houghton Mifflin, 1957), p. 15. (First published 1854).

3. Henry Adams, *Letters*, ed. Ford, vol. 2, p. 178.

4. Ibid., p. 246. Adams liked to play the role of dilettante and at times could give convincing evidence to support it. In 1898 he wrote to Elizabeth Cameron about the war with Spain: "As for the war, it is a God-send to all the young men in America. Even the Bostonians have at last a chance to show that they have emotions" (ibid., p. 178 n.). It is a typical inversion, though mockingly intended. If what is historically right is determined by survival and conquest, what is emotionally valuable must be got by feeding in the stream of history, like the young men of Boston, who are not asked to consider deeply the rightness of the war with Spain.

5. *Democracy* (New York: New American Library, 1961). (First published in 1880.) (Subsequently referred to as *D*.)

6. *Letters*, vol. 2, p. 80.

7. Ernest Samuels, *Henry Adams: The Major Phase*, p. 208; Robert Mane, *Henry Adams on the Road to Chartres*, p. 86.

8. There is no question but that Brooks's work was almost the product of a collaboration with Henry, though it preceded by several years the publication of Henry's major thinking on history and power. Two remarks from Brooks's preface to his book are useful for understanding Henry's view of race:

> The theory proposed [in the book] is based upon the accepted scientific principle that the law of force and energy is of universal application in nature, and that animal life is one of the outlets through which solar energy is dissipated.
>
> Starting from this fundamental proposition, the first deduction is, that, as human societies are forms of animal life, these societies must differ among themselves in energy, in proportion as nature has endowed them, more or less abundantly, with energetic material.

> The evidence . . . seems to point to the conclusion that, when a highly centralized society disintegrates, under the pressure of economic competition, it is because the energy of the race has been exhausted. Consequently, the survivors of such a community lack the power necessary for renewed concentration, and must probably remain inert until supplied with fresh energetic material by the infusion of barbarian blood. [*The Law of Civilization and Decay* (New York: Knopf, 1943), pp. 60, 61. First published in 1896.]

9. Ibid., p. 60.

10. According to Adams, the Jews were international bankers, "goldbugs" well beyond the control of nations and cultures, with no allegiances except to their own

power. They were actually running both sides of the Boer War, which Adams in 1900 saw threatening British dominance. Similarly, while the Jews were behind Chamberlain's power in England, they were at the same time helping the kaiser bring France out of the Atlantic system into an entente with Germany (*Letters*, vol. 2, p. 298).

11. *Letters,* vol. 2, p. 133.

12. Ibid., p. 106. It is significant to see Adams conflate racial and economic identities this way. "The Jew" was often simply his epithet for the financial power ruling the world, but the ease with which he moved between economic and implicit biological forces suggests the melodramatic naturalist allegory that dominated his thought.

13. Ibid., p. 111.

14. Ibid., p. 234.

15. Ibid., p. 241.

16. Ibid., p. 240.

17. Ibid., pp. 230–42.

18. Ibid., p. 234.

19. Ibid., p. 70.

20. Ibid.

21. Ibid., p. 33.

Chapter Five

1. Theodore Dreiser, *Sister Carrie* (Boston: Houghton Mifflin, 1959), p. 6. (First published in 1900.) (Subsequently referred to as *SC.*)

2. Henry David Thoreau, *Walden,* ed. Sherman Paul (Boston: Houghton Mifflin, 1057), p. 15. (First published 1854.)

3. Frank Norris, *McTeague* (San Francisco: Rinehart, 1950), p. 31. (First published in 1900.) (Subsequently referred to as *Mc.*)

4. Ellen Moers gives a full account of Dreiser's friendship with Elmer Gates, during the time he was writing *Sister Carrie,* in *Two Dreisers* (New York: Viking, 1969), pp. 158–69. As an amateur physiological psychologist, Gates seems to have supplied strong evidence for the mechanistic and "chemistic" themes of Dreiser's intellectual life; these were later to be more impressively supported by the work of Jacques Loeb.

5. John Fraser, *Violence in the Arts* (London: Cambridge University Press, 1974), p. 167 n.

6. The more famous instance of Dreiser's need to blur choice is the ambiguous murder in *An American Tragedy,* where Clyde Griffiths literally stumbles into his crime.

7. Frank Norris, *The Octopus* (Boston: Houghton Mifflin, 1958), p. 395. (First published in 1901.) (Subsequently referred to as *O.*)

8. Stephen Crane, *Maggie* (New York: Norton, 1979), p. 6. (First published in 1893.) (Subsequently referred to as *Ma.*)

9. Tony Tanner, in his book on contemporary American fiction, *City of Words* (London: Jonathan Cape, 1971), is one of the first critics I know of to give appropriate stress to themes and effects he calls "the American paranoia": "The possible nightmare of being totally controlled by unseen agencies and powers is never far away in contemporary American fiction" (p. 16). See, particularly, his discussions of Thomas Pynchon and Norman Mailer (ibid., chaps. 7 and 15).

10. Donald Pizer, *Realism and Naturalism in Nineteenth-Century American Literature* (Carbondale, Ill.: Southern Illinois University Press, 1966), pp. 127–31.

11. The modern theme of linking violence with repression came to its most direct expression in the politics of Wilhelm Reich and his literary followers. One of the latter, Norman Mailer, illustrates how compatible this theme is with literary naturalism. The hero of Mailer's famous essay "The White Negro" is the psychopathic victim of society who cures himself by violence. He replaces "a negative and empty fear with an outward action . . . even if the fear is of himself, and the action is to murder. The psychopath murders—if he has the courage—out of the necessity to purge his violence, for if he cannot empty his hatred then he cannot love, his being is frozen with implacable self-hatred for his cowardice" (*Advertisements for Myself,* p. 347).

12. John Dos Passos, *USA* (New York: Random House, 1937), p. 312.

13. Norman Mailer brought these aspects of war-making together in *The Naked and the Dead,* using General Cummings as his archetype. Mailer recognized the latter's fascism as a form of naturalist politics and played vigorously on the themes of power, conflict, and order in the experience of other characters. In this, as in other respects, one can read Mailer's work as the most revealing contemporary expression of traditional naturalist themes.

14. Emile Zola, "Naturalism in the Theatre," in *Documents of Modern Realism,* ed. George J. Becker (Princeton, N.J.: Princeton University Press, 1963), p. 202.

15. Zola, quoted by W. S. Lilly, "The New Naturalism," ibid., p. 280.

16. Guy de Maupassant, "The Lower Elements," ibid., p. 250.

17. Malcolm Cowley, "A Natural History of American Naturalism," ibid., pp. 444–45.

18. See Tony Tanner's excellent discussion of Manichean naturalism in his *City of Words,* pp. 141–52.

19. Norris, as might be expected, provides an illustration of this authoritarian principle: in *The Octopus* the leader of the ranchers, Magnus Derrick, is a magnified man, six feet tall, a cavalry officer with a hawklike nose. The others instinctively look up to him; there was "a certain pride of race in him" (*O* 44). He has the instinct to be master, as others are born to be followers.

20. If greed is fate in Norris's novel, so is instinct. The instinct of the hunted compels McTeague to run for his life, beyond his own choice or sense of direction. He is matched against a fatal process, and finally all that can move him to act on his own behalf is a sixth sense, "an obscure brute instinct," which tells him when he is being pursued and makes him run again (*Mc* 300). It is plausible to invoke a sixth sense against something so mysterious as naturalist fate, the point being that naturalism treats events on a metaphysical scale and can appeal to superstition, despite the initial commitment to empirical science.

21. In Norris's novels these convergences of the dominant political currents of his time are clearly revealed, and they illustrate a relationship difficult to see elsewhere between neo-Darwinian racism, imperialism, and American populist thought.

22. Following is a passage from a classic sociological text, originally published early in this century, in which the imagery of the "People" is also eloquently naturalistic. The authors are writing about the silence of farm workers in England during the nineteenth century, who allowed their experiences to be interpreted solely by upper-class ideologies and spokesmen:

religion, philosophy, and political economy were ready with alleviations and explanations which seemed singularly helpful and convincing to the rich. The voice of the poor themselves does not come to our ears. This great population seems to resemble nature, and to bear all the storms that beat upon it with a strange silence and resignation. But just as nature has her power of protest in some sudden upheaval, so this world of men and women—an underground world as we trace the distance that its voices have to travel to reach us—has a volcanic character of its own, and it is only by some volcanic surprise that it can speak the language of remonstrance or menace or prayer, or place on record its consciousness of wrong. [John L. Hammond and Barbara Hammond, *The Village Labourer* (London: Longmans, 1911), pp. 242–43]

Chapter Six

1. Charles C. Walcutt, in a valuable analysis of *The Octopus,* calls Norris's vitalism "natural dynamism," one branch of the "divided stream" of American naturalism, which is the larger theme of his work (*American Literary Naturalism: A Divided Stream* [Minneapolis: University of Minnesota Press, 1956], p. 146). Walcutt is correct in seeing unresolved inconsistencies, even a radical split, in Norris's view of "nature presented as a conscious, living benign force" and nature presented, as in naturalist tragedy, as a ruthless, overwhelming force, as neutral as it is destructive. However, there is a need to pursue the inner unity of these ideas, or the way in which Norris was groping toward modern forms of resolution, capable of translating natural violence and the experience of ordeal into political and morally redemptive results. It is true that Norris seems to turn back to the rationalizations of laissez-faire competition: the "Wheat" will be harvested and eaten no matter who grows it or whose lives are broken by it. But he could just as easily use the same philosophical stoic considerations to justify revolution and class conflict. And that, too, is noticeable as an interpretation of naturalist process in the dizzy ideological swings of Norris's novel and is what makes it so transparent a guide to the political imagination of his time.

2. For this debate, see R. W. Stallman, ed., *Stephen Crane: An Omnibus* (New York: Knopf, 1952), pp. 223–24.

3. Authority for this statement can be found in the works of one of the best students of modern responses to violence. Hannah Arendt writes as follows:

As far as human experience is concerned, death indicates an extreme of loneliness and impotence. But faced collectively and in action, death changes its countenance; now nothing seems more likely to intensify our vitality than its proximity. Something we are usually hardly aware of, namely, that our own death is accompanied by the potential immortality of the group we belong to and, in the final analysis, of the species, moves into the center of our experience. It is as though life itself, the immortal life of the species, nourished, as it were, by the sempiternal dying of its individual members, is "surging upward," is actualized in the practice of violence. [*On Violence* (New York: Harcourt, Brace & World, 1970), p. 68]

4. Lovejoy, in Lovejoy and Boas, eds., *A Documentary History of Primitivism and Related Ideas,* pp. 9–11.

5. *Thus Spake Zarathustra,* trans. R. S. Hollingdale (Baltimore: Penguin Books, 1962), p. 136.

6. There are strong political analogies here; the therapeutic justifications of political terrorism in the writings of Frantz Fanon come first to mind. The fact that during the civil rights movement his ideas were frequently echoed in statements of the blacks' need to assert self-respecting manhood is general testimony to the popular influence of his thinking. A more complex implication is found in the mood and actions of Israelis since the Holocaust and in the very bitter criticism often directed at the passivity of the Jews before the Nazis, suggesting that there were more virile and noble ways to be slaughtered.

7. Tony Tanner devotes a valuable chapter to apocalyptic moments in contemporary fiction, which he accurately relates to the neoscientific theme of entropy. He lists Norman Mailer, Saul Bellow, John Updike, John Barth, Walker Percy, Stanley

Elkin, and Donald Barthelme among the writers who use both the word and the concept in their works (*City of Words*, pp. 141–52).

8. Jack London, *The Call of the Wild* (New York: Macmillan, 1908), p. 91.

9. Richard Wright, *Native Son* (New York: Harper, 1940), pp. 127, 358. (Ellipsis points are in the original text.)

10. Earlier in *Native Son* this feeling is expressed in Bigger's consciousness as follows:

> He had murdered and had created a new life for himself. It was something that was all his own, and it was the first time in his life he had anything that others could not take from him. [*Native Son*, p. 90]

One may speculate that this motif rides a current in the modern consciousness. I find it present in the dryly passionate lines in Eliot's "Prufrock" that include "There will be time to murder and create," which comes as an outburst against the oppressiveness of quotidian life. And if, in vitalist thought, death can be imagined as the mark left by life-cycles of renewal, why shouldn't murder be creative?

Index